MORE GAMES TEAMS PLAY

ACTIVITIES AND GAMES
FOR POWERING UP
YOUR TEAM'S POTENTIAL

Leslie Bendaly

**McGraw-Hill
Ryerson**

Toronto Montréal New York Burr Ridge Bangkok Bogotá Caracas Lisbon London Madrid
Mexico City Milan New Delhi Seoul Singapore Sydney Taipei

McGraw-Hill
Ryerson Limited

A Subsidiary of The **McGraw·Hill** Companies

ISBN: 0-07-560939-8 (paperback)
ISBN: 0-07-560931-2 (looseleaf)

1234567890 MP 99
Printed and bound in Canada.

Canadian Cataloguing in Publication Data

Bendaly, Leslie
    More games teams play: activities and games for powering up your team's potential

ISBN 0-07-560939-8 (paperback)
ISBN 0-07-560931-2 (looseleaf)

1. Teams in the workplace – Problems, exercises, etc. 2. Personnel management – Problems, exercises, etc. I. Title.

HD66.B45   1999   658.3'128   C99-932364-4

Publisher: **Joan Homewood**
Editorial Co-ordinator: **Catherine Leek**
Production Co-ordinator: **Susanne Penny**
Editor: **Tita Zierer**
Electronic Page Composition: **Kim Monteforte – Heidy Lawrance Associates**
Cover Design: **Steve Eby**

ABOUT THE AUTHOR

Leslie Bendaly, bestselling author, speaker and workshop leader, challenges and inspires organizations, teams and individuals to tap the best of themselves and provides them with the tools they need to realize their goals.

She is a North American leader in the fields of teamwork, group processes, synergistics and peak performance management in environments of change. Leslie is seen as a pioneer in the development of tools and systems for increasing synergy and exceptional performance within teams and across organizations as well as in identifying trends with which individuals and their organizations must be in tune if they are to continue to thrive. Her tools and concepts have been developed and tested through her work with hundreds of organizations from large multinationals such as IBM and Warner Lambert to government and small community organizations.

Her other books include *Strength in Numbers, Games Teams Play, Organization 2000, Winner Instinct* and *The Facilitation Skills Training Kit*. Leslie's work is recognized in *Who's Who in Canada, Who's Who in Canadian Business*, and *Who's Who of Canadian Women*. She is sought after as a facilitator of team development and planning processes.

TABLE OF CONTENTS

Introduction vii

Games for Conferences and Company Meetings xi

Creating a Team Building Workshop xiii

Game Selection Index xix

The Games	Level of Facilitation Skills Required * little experience required *to* *** seasoned skills required	Planning and Preparation * minimal planning time *to* **** approximately 3 to 4 hours	Page Number
Game 1: The Contraption With Attitude	*	****	1
Game 2: Game Time	*	**	23
Game 3: The Treasure of Nephrodite	*	***	39
Game 4: A Little Magic—Version 1	*	**	89
Game 5: A Little Magic—Version 2	*	**	95
Game 6: Ice Floe Adventure	*	***	101
Game 7: Team Slogan	*	*	105
Game 8: It Pays to Advertise	*	*	109
Game 9: Who Done It to the Boss?	*	****	121
Game 10: Living by the Law of Purpose and Passion	*	*	135
Game 11: "I Know What You Did Last Night"	*	*	145
Game 12: The Cabin in the Woods	*	*	147
Game 13: Makes Me Think Of . . .	*	*	153
Game 14: Getting the Point	*	*	159
Game 15: Feelin' Good	*	*	167

The Games	Level of Facilitation Skills Required * little experience required to ****seasoned skills required	Planning and Preparation * minimal planning time to **** approximately 3 to 4 hours	Page Number
Game 16: A Scavenger Hunt for the Eyes	*	***	173
Game 17: Say It in Pictures	*	**	181
Game 18: According To…—Repeat Performance	*	*	187
Game 19: Team Triathlon A	*	*	201
Game 20: Team Triathlon B	*	*	211
Game 21: Team Triathlon C	*	*	223
Game 22: Team Triathlon D	*	*	233
Game 23: Team Triathlon E	*	*	245
Game 24: What Are You Missing?	*	*	257
Game 25: Team Makeover	**	*	267
Game 26: A Letter to Your Team	**	*	269
Game 27: The Pause That Refreshes	**	*	273
Game 28: My Intuition Tells Me	**	*	283
Game 29: The Beauty 4U Dilemma	**	*	293
Game 30: Win As Much As You Can	***	**	303
Game 31: Earthquake	***	*	319
The Updated Team Fitness Test	**	**	333

INTRODUCTION

The original *Games Teams Play* combined a large compendium of activities and games for all types of teams and situations, the "Team Fitness Test" which assesses a team's strengths and opportunities for improvement and provides the framework for a team development process. *More Games Teams Play* both stands on its own and builds on the original. It provides short team games and activities, as well as larger experiential activities.

All games are multi-purpose team building activities. Those that lend themselves particularly well to large corporate events rather than individual team meetings or workshops are described on page xi.

The original "Team Fitness Test" which received so much positive feedback, has been updated and included (see page 333).

HOW TO USE THIS BOOK

Use a single activity or link several together to design a team development workshop. The Game Selection Index (page xix) can assist you in selecting the appropriate game. If planning a team development workshop, consider using the "Team Fitness Test" to check strengths and opportunities for growth. Each activity uses this format:

YOUR SIGN POSTS

- Objectives.
- Time Required.
- Background or Overview (provides the facilitator with greater depth of knowledge and understanding of the game).

- Room Set-up (if applicable).
- Materials Required.
- Preparation (includes detailed instructions and likely responses, including debriefing questions).
- Steps.

 Handouts.

 Game Pieces (materials to be used in the games).

 Transparencies.

 Very Important!

From *More Games Teams Play* by Leslie Bendaly © 2000, McGraw-Hill Ryerson.

TIPS FOR FACILITATORS

This section is meant:

1. For extra support for facilitators who may not have a great deal of experience.
2. As a refresher checklist for others.

Detailed instructions for each game have been given to ensure your success. There are some things, however, as seasoned facilitators know, that cannot be prescribed. A "heads up" has been provided by way of discussing some facilitation success factors.

Be Ready To Go with the Flow (when appropriate)

Each group has a different personality—a game or activity that works well for one might not work as well for another. Although a seasoned facilitator can usually engage a group in most activities and reach anticipated outcomes, occasionally the team personality or individual traits determines whether or not something will work.

I recently worked with a team whose members had enthusiastically contributed throughout the workshop. In one game, "The Treasure of Nephrodite," mini teams were asked to write a short song about why they were the best and to sing it to the game master (the facilitator) which they did and did well. The songs were funny, creative and positive. I wanted a high-spirited, positive wind-up to the day and so concluded by asking each team to sing their song for the whole group. It was quickly evident that several people were uncomfortable with the idea. Although they might reluctantly participate, the workshop would not end on a high.

As I was mentally pulling out some back-up plans, I threw it out to the group for suggestions. The group came to a quick agreement on a celebratory ending that everyone felt good about—simply a boisterous three cheers for the team. A facilitator who is unable to effectively improvise on the spot when something isn't working well can be in real trouble without a back-up plan.

With experience, facilitators gain group intuition. We learn how to "call it." Will this work, won't this work, should I move the group into something that not everyone is immediately excited about, or should I regroup and change directions? There is a fine line between challenging people to stretch themselves and a degree of discomfort that will prevent learning.

Ensuring Success

As there is little growth in the comfort zone, nudging people beyond it is essential and good facilitation ensures a positive experience. However, being able to recognize when even the very best facilitation cannot ensure engagement in and enthusiasm for an activity, is essential.

Success in these situations depends on:

1. The facilitator's confidence based on the knowledge that if something is not working, it is not a reflection of his or her ability. Rather than being critical of a facilitator for changing direction, groups tend to respect the facilitator's ability to do so.

From *More Games Teams Play* by Leslie Bendaly © 2000, McGraw-Hill Ryerson.

2. The facilitator's sharing the responsibility for a successful session with the group. Suggestions as to actively sharing this responsibility follow:
   - During the introduction of the workshop, share with the group something like this: "I will of course make every effort to be in tune with the group to ensure that activities are positive and productive. However, if at any point anyone is not comfortable with something or feels something is not working, please let me know."
   - Check with the group if you sense that something is not working effectively.
   - Warning—be careful not to hand the facilitation over to the group. You are in the role of facilitator because of expertise the group members likely don't have. You want to be flexible but not limp.

3. Having a back-up plan.

Back-up Activities

Many facilitators carry back-up activities or games selected specifically for the group and its objectives. This allows them to redesign the workshop "on the go" as they get a better sense of the group.

Know the Group

Get as much information beforehand about the group so that you can ensure your choice of activities hit the spot.

Sometimes facilitators collect the information but do not use it well, for example, the mix of people, the type of work they do, education, background etc. Such information may indicate what type of activity would most effectively engage the group.

Plan by Visualizing

As you plan the steps you will take and the approach you will use, visualize yourself doing so with the group. Remember to weave in the information you have gathered into the picture you create of the group. It is likely that you will get a strong intuitive sense as to whether something will work well.

Choice of Games

The better you know the team, the easier it is to make the best selection. Some teams find certain games "silly" or a waste of time. We have tried to decrease your risk by providing games that in our experience have been successful with all types of teams—senior or frontline, fun-loving or more serious. However, it is not only important to match the game with the personality of the team, but you as facilitator must enjoy it. If you are not comfortable with it, you won't be able to "get into" it sufficiently to fully engage the team members.

The Importance of Debriefing

Leading a game is pretty simple. When the objective is to team build simply by sharing a "fun" experience, leading the game is all that is required. The challenge for most facilitators is the debriefing—extracting the learning from the experience and applying it to real life.

For each game, as much support as possible is provided with detailed debriefing instructions, including possible debriefing questions and likely responses. You, however, can enrich the process by being observant throughout the game—recognizing behaviors, emotions, challenges, interactions, etc. and addressing them *comfortably* in the debriefing.

You must make judgment calls about the readiness of individuals to be brought personally into the discussion. For example, if you notice that someone is displaying signs of frustration, you might say, *"I sense that some team members were feeling frustrated."* If you are confident that the individual you observed will be comfortable talking about his or her feelings, you might then turn toward that person, smile and say, *"Am I right Kathy?"* If you are not sure, you might add simply, *"Did anyone else sense that as well?"* or *"Am I right?"*

If your observation is a very important one and in order to discuss it, you must directly involve certain group members, you might take them aside at break, describe your observations and ask for their permission to use their experience in the debriefing.

Debriefings should include the following:

1. Sharing the experience. Including any or all of the following:
   - How people felt.
   - How people reacted.
   - What people thought.
2. Identifying the learnings.
3. Transferring the learning to the "real" world.

Using the Games

Many games and activities are multi-purpose. The objectives met will depend on the debriefing. For several games, you are provided with two or more debriefs. You also can choose between debriefing as a group immediately after the game or first giving the mini teams debrief sheets to work through and then discussing their responses in the larger group. Your choice will depend on two variables: time available and the depth of learning desired.

GAMES FOR CONFERENCES AND COMPANY MEETINGS

Many of the experiential activities you will find in *More Games Teams Play* lend themselves well to large company events. A rating is given on the ease of planning for the game, as follows:

- *—little preparation is required.
- ****—a great deal of planning and preparation is necessary.

Ratings as to the required time for a game are given in a range, *e.g.* 1.5 to 2.25 hours. The lower end of the range is the time required to play the game without a debriefing. The higher end is the approximate time required including debriefing.

Top Picks

The following are the top five picks for conferences and company meetings:

DESCRIPTION	EASE OF PLANNING	TIME REQUIRED
Game 3: The Treasure of Nephrodite Teams meet many challenges in their search for the *Treasure of Nephrodite*. Finding the treasure requires a variety of skills, including problem solving, using logic and creativity, and even some mathematical ability. This game ensures that there is something for everyone. The lure of a treasure and the element of competition ensures engagement and fun.	***	1.5—2.5 hours
Game 1: The Contraption With Attitude Teams must build a contraption according to specifications provided and with materials that must be purchased by several means including singing a song, having a team member stand on his or her head and solving brain teasers. Finished contraptions are judged and prizes awarded. This high energy fun requires teamwork and creativity.	****	2—3 hours

DESCRIPTION	EASE OF PLANNING	TIME REQUIRED
Game 16: A Scavenger Hunt for the Eyes Teams must follow a map and look for objects and/or sites en route that provide the answers to a set of rhyming riddles.	***	1.5—2 hours
Game 17: Say It in Pictures Teams are provided with Polaroid cameras and must work as a team to find subjects that represent the team or corporate values, take the photos and create a collage.	**	1.5—2.5 hours
Game 9: Who Done It to the Boss? This highly entertaining game is woven throughout a full day meeting. At the morning kick-off, a video message from the boss is played. It begins very seriously and has attendees slightly on edge and gradually the joke is revealed. A humorous item has been stolen from the boss. Participants are assigned to interrogation teams and given the job of discovering the thief and the hidden article by the end of the day. Each team looks for clues and interrogates witnesses.	****	1 hr. 45 mins. broken into segments throughout the day

CREATING A TEAM BUILDING WORKSHOP

TIPS FOR CREATING AN EFFECTIVE WORKSHOP

- In creating a team building workshop, consider both the development needs and personality of the team. Some teams are more receptive to activities that appeal to the intellect or creativity such as "Team Slogan," rather than an experiential game such as "The Contraption With Attitude" or "Ice Floe Adventure".

    You may use the Game Selection Index as well as information provided in the Table of Contents to select the activities for your workshop.

- Using an instrument such as the "Team Fitness Test" to gather information about the team creates team ownership for the team development process.

    When introducing the topic of team building needs, you can then position the discussion as follows: "According to *your* responses to the "Team Fitness Test," *you* see the following opportunities for growth... Today we will focus on these areas that you have identified as important..."

- Open with a warm-up activity that requires teamwork such as one of the "Team Triathlon" games. On completion of the game, lead a quick discussion as to what the teams did well in the "Triathlon" and how they could have been more effective.

    This creates an effective transition into the discussion of the work teams' opportunities for improvement as identified by the fitness test or other method.

    If there are sensitive issues to be addressed in the workshop, begin with the least sensitive topics. This will give participants an opportunity to increase their comfort level. However, do not leave highly sensitive issues until the very end. There is a danger that there may not be sufficient time to have full dialogue and bring issues to closure. It is also important to end on an upbeat, energetic note.

- Emphasize that team building is not an *event* but a *process*. It is essential that team building continue and that management of the team process be seen as part of the team's task. This means at least stopping periodically, perhaps at a regular team meeting, to examine the team's progress.

- Developing a set of Team Agreements (Handout H0.1), as well as Personal Commitments to Action (Handout H0.2), are essential steps in a successful team building workshop. The Team Agreements also provide a reference point for the ongoing team development process.

Steps for Success

1. Review the observations and learnings from each activity. Invite the team to select the items most important to the team's growth, e.g. "We need to be more sensitive to one another's needs," or "We need to do a better job of sharing the load."

2. Lead the team in developing and committing to a list of Team Agreements. A Team Agreement sheet is provided (H0.1), e.g. We agree to:

   - Check what one another needs regularly.
   - Meet once a week to ensure that the workload is evenly distributed.

   Note: Ensure that agreements are "hard" enough to be measured, i.e. if the team asks, "Are we doing this consistently?" there can be a definite answer. An agreement such as "We agree to be honest and open" is difficult to measure.

3. Ask each member to list their Personal Commitments to Action on the sheet provided in H0.2 and to share one with the whole team. Explain that commitments to action may be big or small actions they will take to contribute even more effectively to the team and to help the team continue to grow.

Handout
H0.1

TEAM AGREEMENTS

- _____

  _____

- _____

  _____

- _____

  _____

- _____

  _____

- _____

  _____

- _____

  _____

- _____

  _____

- _____

  _____

PERSONAL COMMITMENTS TO ACTION

- _____
  _____
  _____
- _____
  _____
  _____
- _____
  _____
  _____
- _____
  _____
  _____
- _____
  _____
  _____
- _____
  _____
  _____
- _____
  _____
  _____
- _____
  _____
  _____
- _____
  _____
  _____

GAME SELECTION INDEX

(according to development need or objective)

Each game offers several benefits. A few are identified here for each game. As you use the games and make them your own, you will find additional outcomes.

	Problem Solving & Decision Making	Communication	Participation	Creativity	Conflict Management	Individual Differences	Cohesiveness	Raising Team Profile	Influencing Skills	Climate/Trust	Giving and Receiving Feedback	Team Spirit/Fun	Getting to Know One Another	Ownership for Team Process and Development
Game 1: The Contraption With Attitude	✓	✓		✓								✓		
Game 2: Game Time	✓		✓	✓								✓		
Game 3: The Treasure of Nephrodite	✓	✓	✓	✓								✓		
Game 4: A Little Magic—Version 1		✓								✓				
Game 5: A Little Magic—Version 2		✓								✓				
Game 6: Ice Floe Adventure	✓	✓	✓	✓			✓					✓	✓	
Game 7: Team Slogan	✓	✓	✓	✓			✓	✓				✓		
Game 8: It Pays to Advertise	✓	✓	✓	✓			✓	✓				✓		
Game 9: Who Done It to the Boss?	✓	✓	✓	✓								✓	✓	
Game 10: Living by the Law of Purpose and Passion	✓	✓					✓						✓	✓
Game 11: "I Know What You Did Last Night"		✓	✓									✓	✓	
Game 12: The Cabin in the Woods	✓	✓	✓	✓								✓		
Game 13: Makes Me Think Of…		✓				✓	✓							
Game 14: Getting the Point	✓	✓												
Game 15: Feelin' Good		✓				✓					✓			
Game 16: A Scavenger Hunt for the Eyes	✓		✓	✓								✓	✓	
Game 17: Say It in Pictures	✓	✓	✓	✓			✓					✓	✓	
Game 18: According To…—Repeat Performance		✓	✓				✓						✓	✓
Game 19: Team Triathlon A	✓	✓	✓									✓	✓	
Game 20: Team Triathlon B	✓	✓	✓									✓	✓	
Game 21: Team Triathlon C	✓	✓	✓									✓	✓	
Game 22: Team Triathlon D	✓	✓	✓									✓	✓	
Game 23: Team Triathlon E	✓	✓	✓									✓	✓	
Game 24: What Are You Missing?	✓	✓	✓											
Game 25: Team Makeover	✓	✓	✓			✓	✓				✓			✓
Game 26: A Letter to Your Team		✓					✓				✓		✓	✓
Game 27: The Pause That Refreshes	✓			✓										
Game 28: My Intuition Tells Me	✓			✓										
Game 29: The Beauty 4U Dilemma	✓	✓	✓		✓	✓	✓		✓		✓			
Game 30: Win As Much As You Can	✓	✓		✓	✓						✓		✓	✓
Game 31: Earthquake	✓	✓	✓		✓	✓	✓				✓		✓	
The Updated Team Fitness Test*														✓

Use the Updated "Team Fitness Test" to identify team strengths and opportunities for growth and to establish an ongoing team development process.

GAME 1 | THE CONTRAPTION WITH ATTITUDE

CHALLENGE: To create a contraption with attitude.

OBJECTIVES

Any or all of the following:

- **To team build.**
- **To tap team creativity.**
- **To demonstrate/practice project planning, management and execution.**
- **To have fun!**

OVERVIEW

Several new twists have been added to an old popular standby activity.

This activity works most easily with teams of up to 10 people, although with good organization and facilitation, larger teams can work well. Teams are challenged to build a contraption that meets certain specifications: it must be able to carry a raw egg from a height of six feet down to the floor, without the egg breaking or cracking and at the same time the contraption must have attitude/personality/flair. Teams are also required to:

- Create a name for their contraption.
- Demonstrate it and make a humorous sales pitch for it.

The facilitator has a store of building material. Team members must purchase the materials they wish to use. Payments for various materials include:

- Solving a set of brain teasers.
- Singing a song (Choose something popular. When the Macarena was hot, we used that song.)
- One team member must stand on their head for 10 seconds.
- Solving a riddle.

Your Notes

From *More Games Teams Play* by Leslie Bendaly © 2000, McGraw-Hill Ryerson.

The team will work through five steps:

1. Design.
2. Development including purchase of materials.
3. Testing and fine-tuning.
4. Selecting a name and writing a promotional piece.
5. Presentation—"unveiling" of the contraption, including announcing its name, presenting the promotional piece (jingle, sales pitch) and demonstrating its capability.

For added fun, you may allow the teams to judge each other's contraptions and award prizes. This game also provides a great photo opportunity—a chance to capture team members having fun. Some organizations videotape the presentations.

TIME REQUIRED: 2.5 hours (approximately)

You can adjust the times given to suit your program and number of participants. The following is usually adequate:

Activity	Time Required
Getting organized	10 minutes
Contraption design (including checking out materials available)	30 minutes
Building (including purchasing material)	45 minutes
Testing and fine-tuning	15 minutes
Creating and writing a promotional piece	20 minutes
Presentations and judging, depending on number of teams	5 to 7 minutes per team

ROOM SET-UP AND PLANNING

- The room must provide plenty of working space for each team. Ideally, the room will have an easy to clean floor (in the event of broken eggs). If not, plan for how the floor can be protected.

Your Notes

- Plan the physical set-up. Where is the best place for the store (where participants will purchase their material)? Where can the teams promote their contraption so that everyone can see? Can people gather around the spot where the team is working or can the contraption be moved to a staging area?

MATERIALS REQUIRED

- Eggs (two or three per team in case of accidents in testing stage).
- Tubing (different lengths).
- Markers.
- Paper clips.
- Styrofoam cups.
- Glue.
- Duct tape.
- Wooden dowels.
- Elastics.
- String.
- Streamers.
- Wooden sticks.
- Salt and paper towel (to clean up any broken eggs).

PREPARATION

- Purchase the material.
- Check that the venue works for this activity. You need lots of space and must be able to allow for the occasional broken egg.
- Select a riddle to be solved and song to be sung during the Purchase List (Handout H1.4).
- Identify judges and communicate with them. Distribute and discuss the Judging Sheet H1.7.
- Depending on the number of people involved, you may want to assign assistant facilitators (approximately three teams per facilitator) to assist you in conducting the activity.

TIP

Sprinkling plenty of salt on a broken egg allows easy clean-up.

Your Notes

Note: The approach you take to both the introduction to the activity and the debriefing will of course depend on your objectives. Although most client organizations are looking for a combination of fun and learning, there is often more weight on one or the other. You have the choice of several debriefs from light to intensive. You might opt for no debriefing if your main objective is to have fun and are not concerned about transferring learning to the workplace.

STEPS

1. Introduction. If this is to be a "fun only" event, present a brief, energetic introduction which is appropriate to the group and then describe the activity.

2. Distribute Handouts H1.1 to H1.2 and review the information in detail.

3. Conduct the activity (Handout H1.4). Circulate among the teams, cheer them on and help keep the energy level high. Facilitate the presentations and judging.

4. Lead the debriefing. You may want to develop your own debrief to match your specific objectives. A couple of debriefs follow (Handouts H1.5 and H1.6). You may choose to do a light debrief by simply discussing the questions provided on the handout with the group. For a more intensive debriefing, you may ask the individual teams to discuss the questions and bring their observations to the larger group. In either case, you might wind up with: "Which of the learnings from this activity are most relevant back on the job?" Capture the key points on an overhead transparency, flip chart or electronically.

Your Notes

From *More Games Teams Play* by Leslie Bendaly © 2000, McGraw-Hill Ryerson.

CHALLENGE: TO CREATE A CONTRAPTION WITH ATTITUDE

Your team must build a contraption that will carry an uncooked egg from a height of six feet down to the floor without the egg breaking or cracking. It must be a freestanding structure.

Your objective is to create a contraption that meets the above specifications and at the same time has personality/attitude/flair.

You will be asked to name your contraption and to write a brief sales pitch for it. Make it fun. For example, you might write a limerick or a song.

Your contraption will be judged on the following:

1. Its functionality (meets the specifications).

2. Its attitude/personality/creativity.

3. Your sales pitch.

Have fun!

CONTRAPTION INSTRUCTIONS

You have two hours to complete the following steps:

1. Get organized.

2. Design your contraption.

3. Purchase your materials by solving riddles, brain teasers etc.

4. Build your contraption.

5. Test and fine-tune your contraption.

6. Write a brief sales pitch for your contraption (no longer than 30 seconds in length).

7. Practice your demonstration and presentation. Be prepared to present your contraption to the larger group.

CONTRAPTION DESIGN

SPECIFICATIONS

Your contraption must be able to carry an egg from a height of six feet down to the floor without breaking or cracking. It must be a freestanding structure. It must have personality/attitude/flair.

MATERIALS

You may use all or any of the materials noted in the Contraption Purchase List (H1.4) in the design of the contraption. You will also want to check the purchase cost as there is time and talent involved in making some of the purchases. Outside materials are not permitted.

Handout
H1.4

THE CONTRAPTION PURCHASE LIST

MATERIALS	COST
Tubing	Solve a set of brain teasers.
Duct tape	Sing the song requested by your Facilitator.
Wooden dowels	One team member must stand on their head for 10 seconds.
Egg	Solve a riddle.

String
Streamers
Elastics
Paper clips
Markers

➡ No charge.

DEBRIEF PROJECT MANAGEMENT

TIME REQUIRED: 30 minutes

In this activity, you managed a project from conception to completion.

1. What do you believe were your greatest strengths as a team? (What did you do very well?)

2. What strengths did each member bring to the process?

3. If you were to start over again, what would you do differently? What changes would you make to the process or the way in which you managed the activity?

4. Identify points that also apply to managing projects on the job.

DEBRIEF TEAMWORK

Individually answer the following questions:

1. Identify the roles each team member played or what each person brought to the activity.

2. Was it easy to come to agreement on the various decisions that had to be made? Why or why not?

3. What were your greatest strengths as a team?

4. How could your teamwork have been enhanced? Give examples.

5. What did you bring to the team?

Share your responses with your team.

JUDGING THE CONTRAPTION

Please allot points (based on a rating of 1 to 5 where 1 is low and 5 is high) based on the following factors:

1. Meets specifications.

   The contraption must be able to carry an uncooked egg from a height of six feet down to the floor without the egg breaking or cracking. It must be a freestanding structure.

   1   2   3   4   5

2. Ingenuity of mechanical design.

   1   2   3   4   5

3. Creativity of design (i.e. demonstration of personality/attitude).

   1   2   3   4   5

4. Marketing:

   (a) Sales pitch—originality/creativity.

   1   2   3   4   5

   (b) Presentation of contraption and sales pitch.

   1   2   3   4   5

BRAIN TEASERS

1.

2. youitsme

3.

i   o

v s n

i

4. without wocarerld

BRAIN TEASERS— ANSWERS

1. Joke around

2. It's between you and me

3. Distorted vision

4. Without a care in the world

GAME 2 | GAME TIME

OBJECTIVES

One or all of the following:

- ▓ **To demonstrate team skills and attitudes.**
- ▓ **To examine one's personal response to constructive criticism.**
- ▓ **To better understand how to effectively influence others.**
- ▓ **To have fun.**

TIME REQUIRED: Two hours

MATERIALS REQUIRED

- Dice (two per group).
- Bingo chips (handful per group).
- Bristol board (one sheet per group).
- Markers (at least two colours per group).
- Plastic cups (one per group).

OVERVIEW

In this activity, participants work in groups of six to 10 people (ideally) to create a new, original game. Each group judges another group's game. Each group then has the opportunity to improve their game (referred to as game enhancement) with input from a member of the team that judged them.

Phase 1

The first phase of game development depends on teamwork and the use of creativity and generates fun.

Phase 2

In Phase 2, groups test each other's products and present ideas for improvement.

Your Notes

Phase 3

Phase 3 is the game enhancement phase in which teams use feedback to improve their game. Phases 2 and 3 illustrate how great the sense of pride and ownership is for something one has energetically participated in creating. That pride of ownership produces positive energy and enthusiasm but can also prevent the owners from openly receiving input or seeing better ways of doing things.

Phase 4

Presentation of winners.

See Instructions (Handout H2.1) for more details.

STEPS

1. Distribute the Instructions (Handout H2.1) and materials.

2. Review the Instructions in Handout H2.1.

3. Phase 1—Teams create a game within the one hour time limit.

4. Phase 2—Allow 30 minutes for testing and feedback. Groups are paired so that one group will demonstrate their game, and another group is assigned to be their testing team. The testing team will play the game, discuss its pros and cons and give recommendations for improvement (time allotted is 15 minutes). Teams then change roles and the teams that had been testers, now demonstrate their game and the other group becomes the testers. Keep in mind that a group that has received critical remarks may tend to be overly tough in retaliation. You may decide to have teams switch partners.

5. Phase 3—Teams make adjustments to their games incorporating the other team's feedback (time allotted 10 minutes).

6. Phase 4—Groups are invited to demonstrate their games. The games will be judged by all other groups and scores

Your Notes

tallied. If there are five or fewer groups, each game is demonstrated to the whole group. If there are more, break into smaller clusters of groups for judging and have a winner for each cluster. Use "Game Evaluation Sheet", Handout H2.2. You may need more than one sheet depending on the number of teams.

7. Share results and declare a winner. You might announce it as the next Monopoly or Trivial Pursuit.

8. Conduct one or both of the following debriefing, depending on your time and your key objectives. If you are conducting both, you might insert Debrief A after Step 3 (game creation).

Debrief A

(a) Distribute the Teamwork Debrief (Handout H2.3).

(b) Ask each group to discuss and respond to the questions on the Teamwork Debrief handout (time allotted 20 – 30 minutes).

(c) Ask each group to share their responses.

(d) Recap key learning points that emerge.

These are likely to include:

- Some individuals' over-enthusiasm may hinder full participation.
- Good ideas can be lost if the process isn't managed. (You might discuss the advantages of having an appointed leader or facilitator.)
- Jumping too quickly to a decision can limit its potential success (insufficient input/discussion/ideas).

Debrief B

(a) Distribute Receiving Feedback Debrief (Handout H2.4).

(b) Ask each group to discuss and respond to the questions posed on the debrief sheet.

Your Notes

(c) Invite groups to share their observations with the larger group.

(d) Extract and recap key learning points. These should include:

- Pride of ownership creates positive energy.
- Ownership of a concept can make it difficult to listen openly to suggestions for improvement.
- The way constructive suggestions are presented influences our receptivity.
- People who are not involved in a project can bring new and important perspectives to it.

Your Notes

CREATING THE GAME

ALLOTTED TIME: one hour

Your task is to create a new and exciting game that has the potential to compete with the most popular games on the market.

You may use all or any of the materials provided. You may add other materials if they are easily at your disposal.

You must:

1. Design a game complete with rules.

2. Name the game.

3. Be prepared to demonstrate the game. (Keep in mind you want to "sell" your game as the best.)

EVALUATION

Each of the four criteria will be rated on a 1 to 5 scale where 1 is a low score and 5 is a high score, for a possible total score of 20.

You will be judged on the following:

1. The game's engagement factor (is it interesting?).

2. Its fun factor.

3. Its name (is it catchy?).

4. Your originality/creativity.

GAME EVALUATION SHEET

Rate each criteria on a 1 to 5 scale where 1 is a low score and 5 is a high score.

Aspect evaluated \ Team Name	Team	Team	Team
Engagement factor (is it interesting?)			
Fun Factor			
Name (is it catchy?)			
Originality/creativity			

TEAMWORK DEBRIEF

The purpose of this debrief is to gain insight and learning from the activity. Look for your strengths and celebrate them. Note, however, that the greatest learning will come from identifying ways in which you could have worked even more effectively.

Therefore challenge one another's thinking when responding to the following questions.

CREATIVITY

1. How did you generate game ideas? Did you have a plan or structure for generating ideas?

2. Did everyone participate in idea generation?

3. Were any ideas lost or not explored thoroughly enough?

4. Was there building on ideas?

5. Identify behaviors that promoted creativity.

6. Identify behaviors that stifled and limited creativity.

(continued)

TEAM DECISION-MAKING

1. Did you have a method for selecting a game idea?

2. Did you have consensus on the choice?

3. Was everyone enthusiastic about the choice?

4. Did anyone take the lead in bringing the decision to closure?

5. Did everyone participate fully?

If everyone did not participate fully, why not? Possible factors may have been that:

• Some people were stronger idea generators.

• Some people were more verbal and took the lead.

• People with quieter styles were at a disadvantage.

• Other reasons.

IMPLEMENTATION—CREATING THE GAME

1. How did the team work to develop the idea into a game?

2. Did someone take an organizational or leadership role?

3. Was someone the motivator?

4. Was it easy to come to agreement on the details, e.g. the rules?

5. What were your strengths at this stage?

6. What were your opportunities for improvement?

RECEIVING FEEDBACK DEBRIEF

Individually answer the following questions and then discuss them in your group.

1. How did you **feel** about the input: positive; excited; defensive; frustrated, etc.?

2. What did you **think** about the input? Possible perceptions might include:

   • It would enhance the game.

   • It was not useful.

   • The person giving input didn't understand why we had made certain choices.

   • _____

   _____

3. If you felt some discomfort with the input, what could the evaluator have done to increase your receptivity?

   _____

   _____

   _____

(continued)

If you felt positively about the input, what did the evaluator do to help you feel that way?

_____

_____

_____

_____

4. What else affected your receptivity to the input?

_____

_____

_____

_____

5. What did you gain from receiving the evaluator's outside perspective?

_____

_____

_____

_____

GAME 3 THE TREASURE OF NEPHRODITE

OBJECTIVES

One or all of the following:

- ▨ **To team build.**
- ▨ **To better appreciate each others' skills and abilities.**
- ▨ **To have fun.**

TIME REQUIRED: 1.5 hours

OVERVIEW

In The Treasure of Nephrodite, teams become archaeological teams in search of an ancient treasure. They must escape from a locked chamber; interpret a message from the Sphinx; meet a variety of challenges (which test reasoning, verbal, mathematical, creative and communication skills); and solve clues to find the treasure.

MATERIALS REQUIRED

- Game Instructions (Handouts H3.1 and H3.4).
- Game Pieces G3.1 to G3.7.
- Oranges—one per group.
- Envelopes: five per group.
- Masking tape and scissors.
- The Treasure—ideally chocolate coins wrapped in gold foil. If not available, any candy will do. Some companies opt for more extravagant treasures.
- Treasure Chest—a container that looks as much like a treasure chest as possible.

Your Notes

STEPS

1. Distribute the instruction sheets (Handout H3.1). Explain to the group that should they have a problem they should "just ask" (the importance of this is evident when you reach the end of the game). Set up the game by describing the scenario set out in the instructions. Explain that they will be required to successfully face several challenges in order to find the treasure. As they complete each challenge, they will find written instructions for the next challenge. *Note:* For answers to each challenge, see page 47.

2. Conduct the game as presented in the following Game Description.

GAME DESCRIPTION

The Treasure of Nephrodite creates a great deal of fun and energy. It combines puzzle solving, the need for interaction and team-work, the use of logic and creativity, with the appeal of competition and treasure. How the game is led depends on the size of the group. Two roles must be filled: that of the Guardian of the Treasure and the Oracle. If the group has 40 members or less, the facilitator can play both roles. For a larger group, it is recommended that you have someone else take the role of the Oracle.

Part of the excitement is created by the need for members of the teams to run to the facilitator, Guardian or Oracle for clues or next steps.

The following step by step description will help you become familiar with the various components of the game.

1. The group is divided into teams of 6 to 8 members.

2. Participants receive the following information (Handout H3.1):

   You are part of an archaeological team. You have discovered the burial site of Queen Nephrodite in a pyramid in the

Your Notes

Your Notes

ancient city of Memphis. While exploring the tomb, you have become locked in a chamber.

There is little oxygen. You must find a way to get out of the chamber quickly. You also are determined to find the treasure you are sure is somewhere in the pyramid.

Other archaeological teams are also locked in the chamber. Each team not only wants to get out, but wants to be the first to reach the treasure.

There is one exit from the chamber, an opening that is 30 feet above your head.

A rope ladder is hanging down from the opening, but several rungs have rotted away. You must repair the three rungs. To learn how to repair them, open Envelope 1.

3. **Envelope 1** (G3.1)

You must repair the three rungs of the ladder in order to climb out of the chamber. To repair the first rung, insert the missing number.

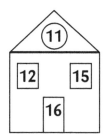 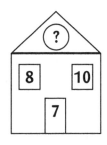

To repair the second rung, find the letter that will turn each of the words into a new word.

☐ **ROW   HOST**
  RIP   OAT

To repair the third rung, insert the word that completes the first word and begins the second.

PASS☐**LESS**

Check your answers (on page 47) with the Game Master. If they are correct, you can successfully climb out of the chamber. Go to Envelope 2.

4. **Envelope 2**

The Second Chamber

You have climbed up the ladder to find yourself in a second chamber. It has a sealed doorway. To get through this doorway, you must have one chisel, one hammer, one crowbar and a flashlight. Check your toolbox. If any items are missing, you must obtain them. When you get out, go to the envelope marked "The Oracle."

Note to facilitators: Place inside Envelope 2 a smaller envelope marked Tool Kit. In this envelope, place the four tools (G3.3). Instead of providing one of each type, organize the envelopes so that each has two of one tool and one each of two other tools, e.g. two chisels, one hammer and one flashlight. Each group then will be missing one tool and must recognize that they must trade their duplicate with another group to get the tool they need.

More instructions on how to organize the envelopes will follow later.

5. **Envelope 3** marked The Oracle.

Envelope 3 contains the following (Game Piece G3.4):

The Oracle

Congratulations! You have gotten out of the tomb. As you exit, you see the Oracle. You are certain it has information to help you find your way out. You must give the Oracle an offering. Solve the puzzle to find out what the offering is and give it to the Oracle.

Your Notes

From *More Games Teams Play* by Leslie Bendaly © 2000, McGraw-Hill Ryerson.

Offering to the Oracle

Unscramble the words to learn what you must offer the Oracle.

d s g o   _ _ _ ⊖

m d o i s w   ⊖ _ _ _ _ _

s r e e t d   _ ⊖ _ ⊖ _ _

b m o t   ⊖ _ _ _

x i n p h s   ⊖ _ _ _ _ _

Offer the Oracle

_ _ _ _ _ _

When the message has been deciphered, the participants realize they must offer the Oracle something sweet. This gives them several options—a candy, sugar from the coffee table, gum, etc.

6. Message from the Oracle

When the group member offers the Oracle a sweet, the Oracle in return gives the participant an orange and mysteriously says "find the message within." You will have inserted a message inside the orange (instructions to follow)* but at first participants usually look for a deeper meaning rather than taking the message literally and actually looking inside the orange.

The message inside the orange reads:

Message from the Oracle

You are about to meet the Guardian of the Treasure. You must convince her that you deserve her help because you are an excellent team.

She likes music. Therefore, you must write a short song about why your team deserves her help and sing it to her.

---

*Instructions for Inserting the Message into the Orange
Copy the Message G3.5 (one copy per group). Roll each set of instructions and wrap in tin foil. Insert a sharp, pointed knife into the navel of each orange. Insert foil wrapped instructions into the slit.

Your Notes

---

7. After each group sings to the Guardian of the Treasure, give them The Zin Obelisk Challenge—Group Instruction Sheet (Handout H3.2) and Game Pieces G3.6. The Game Pieces, cut from G3.6, (the Zin Obelisk information pieces) should be divided equally between the team members. Caution members not to read one another's information. *Note:* If you wish to shorten the game you can omit this challenge. Teams are allowed a maximum of 25 minutes to complete the Zin Obelisk Challenge.

The Zin Obelisk Challenge*— Group Instruction Sheet

In the ancient city of Atlantis, a solid, rectangular obelisk, called a zin, was built in honor of the Queen Nephrodite. The structure took less than two weeks to complete.

The task of your team is to determine on which day of the week the obelisk was completed. You have 25 minutes for this task.

You will be given pieces of information related to the task. Divide the pieces of information equally among your team members. Share the information and questions orally with your teammates. You may not show your information to other participants.

8. If any group has not obtained the answer within 25 minutes, you might give them some clues. Since other groups are now well ahead of them, no one minds the stragglers receiving a little help. When participants bring the correct answer (Neptiminus) to you, give them the final clue—"Find the Tree of Wisdom." This is the fifth challenge. *Note:* Because it is presented orally, there is no game piece for Challenge 5.

*Original source: Mike Woodcock.

Your Notes

At the end of the game you might share the answer and rationale with the whole group (Handout H3.3).

9. You will have stuck their final clue instructions (Just Ask—Game Piece G3.7) to a tree if you have easy access to a treed area. If not, find somewhere else to post or place the final clue and change your reference #8 in the Tree of Wisdom to something else.

10. The Game Master gives the treasure to the first group who JUST ASKS for it. You might decide to have one or two smaller, runner-up treasures.

DEBRIEF

You might choose to use this exercise as a "just for fun" team builder with no formal debrief. Choose from the two options below.

Option A

For an intense debrief use the Debrief Journal (Handout H3.4).

1. Ask participants to take 10 minutes to individually reflect on the activity and then to discuss their responses with their team (30 minutes in total).

2. Invite teams to share their responses and observations.

3. Identify learnings.

4. Discuss how the learning can be applied at work.

5. Recap key learning points.

Option B

For a shorter debrief, discuss the debriefing questions in the larger group, identify and recap key learnings. Key learning points usually include:

1. The need to ensure full participation. A common experience in this game is to have a few members of a team take charge and drive the outcome. This is partly due to the elements of competition and time

urgency that are part of the game. You might note to the group that these are also elements of the "real" world.

2. Effective communication is critical when a team is at work, whatever the task.

3. Different members have different skills and aptitudes. It is important to fully tap them.

4. Having a common goal we are all excited about is a huge motivator.

Your Notes

THE TREASURE OF NEPHRODITE—ANSWERS

First Rung

Insert the missing number.

11—Subtracting the number on the door from the sum of the numbers in the windows gives the number on the roof.

Second Rung

Insert the missing letter.

G ROW HOST
RIP OAT

G is the only letter if added to the beginning of each word will turn each of the words into a new word.

Third Rung

Insert the word that completes the first word and begins the second.

PASS AGE LESS

Offering to the Sphinx

sweets

Your Notes

GAME INSTRUCTIONS

You are part of an archaeological team. You have discovered the burial site of Queen Nephrodite in a pyramid in the ancient city of Memphis. While exploring the tomb, you have become locked in a chamber.

There is little oxygen. You must find a way to get out of the chamber quickly. You also are determined to find the treasure you are sure is somewhere in the pyramid.

Other archaeological teams are also locked in the chamber. Each team not only wants to get out, but wants to be the first to reach the treasure.

There is one exit from the chamber, an opening that is 30 feet above your head.

A rope ladder is hanging down from the opening, but several rungs have rotted away. You must repair the three rungs. To learn how to repair them, open Envelope 1.

Handout
H3.2

THE ZIN OBELISK CHALLENGE— GROUP INSTRUCTION SHEET

Beside the tomb of Queen Nephrodite stands a solid, rectangular obelisk, called a zin, which was built in her honor. The structure took less than two weeks to complete.

The task of your team is to determine on which day of the week the obelisk was completed. You have 25 minutes for this task.

You will be given pieces of information related to the task to help you organize the information. You may share this information orally, but you may not show your information to other participants.

THE ZIN OBELISK CHALLENGE

The answer is **Neptiminus**.

RATIONALE

1. The dimensions of the zin indicate that it contains 50,000 cubic feet of stone blocks.

2. The blocks are one cubic foot each, therefore, 50,000 blocks are required.

3. Each worker works seven schlibs in a day (two schlibs are devoted to rest).

4. Each worker lays 150 blocks per schlib, therefore each worker lays 1,050 blocks per day.

5. There are eight workers per day, therefore 8,400 blocks are laid per working day.

6. The 50,000th block, therefore, is laid on the sixth working day.

7. Since work does not take place on Daydoldrum, the sixth working day is Neptiminus.

DEBRIEF JOURNAL

Respond to the following individually. When you are finished, share your observations with your team members.

1. What did you like most about playing the game?

_____

_____

_____

_____

_____

2. What did you like least?

_____

_____

_____

_____

_____

(continued)

3. Consider how your team members worked together during the game and rate the following statement on a 1 to 10 scale, where 1 is a low score and 10 is a high score.

Everyone participated fully in the activity.

1 2 3 4 5 6 7 8 9 10

If you chose a rating of 6 or less, why do you believe the participation was limited?

_____

_____

_____

_____

_____

If you chose a rating of 7 or more, what factors encouraged full participation?

_____

_____

_____

_____

_____

(continued)

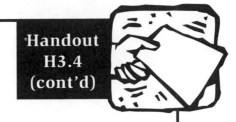

4. What did everyone bring to the game? List each of your team members' names and beside each, jot down a contribution he or she made. The contribution could be in the form of a role (e.g. leader, organizer, cheerleader); a skill or aptitude (e.g. an ability to solve brain teasers); or an attitude (e.g. they stayed positive when the rest were ready to give up).

Name	**Contribution**

(continued)

KEY LEARNING POINTS

CHALLENGE 1

You must repair the three rungs of the ladder in order to climb out of the chamber. To repair the first rung, insert the missing number.

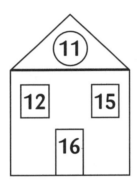

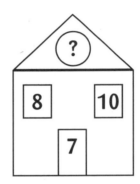

To repair the second rung, find the letter that will turn each of the words into a new word.

ROW   HOST
RIP   OAT

To repair the third rung, insert the word that completes the first word and begins the second.

PASS[____]LESS

Check your answers with the Game Master. If they are correct, you can successfully climb out of the chamber. Go to Envelope 2, The Second Chamber.

CHALLENGE 2

THE SECOND CHAMBER
You have climbed up the ladder to find yourself in a second chamber. It has a sealed doorway. To get through this doorway, you must have one chisel, one hammer, one crowbar and a flashlight. Check your toolbox. If any items are missing, you must obtain them. When you get out, go to the envelope marked Challenge 3, "The Oracle."

Game Piece G3.3

TOOL KIT

Hammer	Hammer	Hammer
Hammer	Hammer	Chisel
Chisel	Chisel	Chisel

(continued)

Chisel	**Crowbar**

Crowbar	**Crowbar**	**Crowbar**

Crowbar	**Flashlight**	**Flashlight**

Flashlight	**Flashlight**	**Flashlight**

**Game
Piece
G3.4**

CHALLENGE 3

THE ORACLE

Congratulations! You have gotten out of the chamber. As you exit, you see the Oracle. You are certain it has information to help you find your way out. You must give the Oracle an offering. Solve the puzzle to find out what offering is required. Then get the offering and give it to the Oracle.

Offering to the Oracle

Unscramble the words to learn what you must offer the Oracle.

d s g o ⎯ ⎯ ⎯ ◯

m d o i s w ◯ ⎯ ⎯ ⎯ ⎯ ⎯ ⎯

s r e e t d ⎯ ◯ ⎯ ◯ ⎯ ⎯

b m o t ◯ ⎯ ⎯ ⎯

x i n p h s ◯ ⎯ ⎯ ⎯ ⎯ ⎯

Offer the Oracle

⎯ ⎯ ⎯ ⎯ ⎯ ⎯

Game
Piece
G3.5

CHALLENGE 4

The message inside the orange reads:

Message from the Oracle

You are about to meet the Guardian of the Treasure. You must convince her that you deserve her help because you are an excellent team.

She likes music. Therefore, you must write a short song about why your team deserves her help and sing it to her.

THE ZIN OBELISK CHALLENGE

The basic measurement of time is a day.

A day is divided into schlibs and ponks.

The length of the zin is 50 feet.

The height of the zin is 100 feet.

(continued)

The width of the zin is 10 feet.

The zin is built of stone blocks.

Each block is one cubic foot.

Day 1 of the week is called Aquaday.

Day 2 of the week is called Neptiminus.

(continued)

Day 3 of the week is called Sharkday.

Day 4 of the week is called Mermaidday.

Day 5 of the week is called Daydoldrum.

There are five days in a week.

The working day has nine schlibs.

(continued)

Game
Piece
G3.6
(cont'd)

Each worker takes rest periods during the working day totaling 16 ponks.

There are eight ponks in a schlib.

At any time when work is taking place, there is a gang of nine people on site.

One member of each gang has religious duties and does not lay blocks.

No work takes place on Daydoldrum.

(continued)

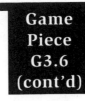

Game Piece G3.6 (cont'd)

A cubitt is a cube, all sides of which measure one megalithic yard.

There are 3½ feet in a megalithic yard.

The zin is made up of green blocks.

Green has special religious significance on Mermaidday.

Each gang includes two women.

(continued)

Work starts at daybreak on Aquaday.

Only one gang is working on the construction of the zin.

There are eight gold scales in a gold fin.

Each block costs two gold fins.

Workers each lay 150 blocks per schlib.

Game
Piece
G3.7

CHALLENGE 6

Remember the words of your Facilitator.

JUST ASK!

GAME 4 A LITTLE MAGIC Version 1

OBJECTIVE

■ To examine the level of team trust.

■ To develop agreements to strengthen trust.

TIME REQUIRED: 50 minutes +

BACKGROUND

Trainers and facilitators know the benefit of linking a picture to a point they wish a group to remember. A magic trick is a dramatic way to create a picture that won't be forgotten and if you link it well to the point you are making, neither will the message.

In this activity, the empty glass magic trick is used to introduce an examination of trust in the team.

MATERIALS REQUIRED

• Slush or gel powder (available at magic stores).

• Styrofoam cups.

STEPS

1. Pick up a styrofoam cup (already filled with the slush or gel powder as per instructions on the package) and hold it up so everyone can see it.

2. Pour water from a clear jug or bottle so that the water can be seen easily by those farthest away.

3. Ask the group "What did I just do?" The likely answer will be "you poured water into the cup." Then say something like "I know this sounds like a question with an obvious answer, but 'What is in the cup?'" At this stage, since people are not

---

Your Notes

---

expecting magic tricks, the likely answer is "water." (If anyone suspects something and answers "nothing" or gives another response, you can simply move into the trust topic more quickly with a comment such as "You mean if I said there was water in the cup, you would not believe me?")

Continue with "If I were to tell you there was no water in this cup, even though you saw me pour it in, would you believe me?" At least some if not all members of the group will say "no!"

Finish up by asking "Isn't there anyone who trusts me when I say this is empty?" Select someone who says they trust you. Ask him or her to come up and sit on a chair at the front of the room. Then ask if he or she trusts you enough to let you tip the cup over their head. If the answer is yes, slowly tip the cup over their head. Angle it so that participants cannot easily see inside it. However, since the solidified slush is translucent it is not easily noticed. If the first candidate says no, look for another. If you cannot find one, you can tip it over your own head.

4. You might begin a discussion of trust by saying jokingly: "I can't *believe* that people didn't trust *me* of all people." Or if you prefer, start with the next question "Why didn't you trust me when I said there was no water in the cup?"

Likely responses:

- We saw you pour the water. Logic told us there was water in the cup.
- We don't know you well.
- We haven't tested whether we could trust you before.
- No one wanted to take the risk.
- It was easier not to trust than to risk getting wet.

5. Continue the exercise by asking, "Do these trust issues ever arise in your team?"

Your Notes

There will likely be at least a few nods. Continue, "I'd like you to think about that a little more in your workshop groups." Distribute Handout H4.1.

6. Review the instructions and allow 25 minutes for discussion.

7. Depending on the time available, you may have groups share their responses to each question or focus only on the last question. Ask, "What do you believe your team members should do to enhance the level of trust in your team?"

8. Facilitate the identification of points which everyone in the group supports (preferably no more than 5).

9. Invite the team to turn these points into team agreements. For example, if an agreed upon point read "we should check the facts before we jump to conclusions," the team agreement might then read "we agree to check the facts and not jump to conclusions."

Handout
H4.1

WORKOUT: A LITTLE MAGIC

TIME REQUIRED: 25 minutes

Something that is real magic is trust. Trust dramatically changes the team experience and team performance.

In your workshop groups, appoint a discussion leader and have each of the group members respond to the following questions:

1. How strong do you believe the element of trust is in your team? (Rate individually from 1 to 10, where 1 is low and 10 is very high.) Share and discuss your ratings within your group.

2. As a group, identify and discuss what team members could do to increase the level of trust.

3. Be prepared to share three recommendations with the larger group.

GAME 5 A LITTLE MAGIC Version 2

OBJECTIVES

One or all of the following:

- ■ **To increase participants' awareness of the fact that "things are not always as they appear."**
- ■ **To heighten participants' recognition of assumptions they make and how those assumptions lead to misunderstanding and often conflict.**

TIME REQUIRED: 50 minutes +

OVERVIEW

In this activity, the empty glass magic trick (as described in Game 4: A Little Magic—Version 1) is used to introduce an examination of assumptions and how they can lead to conflict.

STEPS

1. Follow the steps in Game 4: "A Little Magic—Version 1" until the end of Step 3 and then continue as follows.

2. Ask the group "Would you agree that what appears to be is not necessarily so? You saw me pour water into the cup—a logical conclusion would therefore seem to be that there is water in the cup. What appeared to be was not true. It was an illusion.

   "Illusion also plays a key role in the workplace. It contributes to misunderstanding and conflict. We often see a behavior and attach a conclusion to it that is often completely wrong. We make assumptions."

Your Notes

3. Describe a scenario in which a team member made an assumption about another's behavior that led to conflict. The following example is one that you might use if you don't have one you feel is appropriate.

SAMPLE SCENARIO

Situation

Kathy, Carol and Jim had talked over coffee about telephone coverage at breaks. They found that the system they were using now was not effective and they had some ideas for improvement.

A team meeting was booked for the next day and they agreed to raise the issue. Carol was nervous because she was not comfortable speaking up in meetings and they all realized that some team members would likely not agree with them. They agreed to all speak, share their ideas and support one another.

In the meeting, Carol found an opening in the discussion and raised their issue. Jim quickly followed up with his thoughts.

They both looked to Kathy but she was looking down at the table and said nothing. When they paused, someone else raised another subject and their concern was never dealt with. Kathy left the meeting quickly.

"Well, thanks a lot." Carol said under her breath, watching Kathy leave.

Jim followed Carol out of the room. "We sure got a lot of help there didn't we?"

"It looks like Kathy is all talk," Carol responded. "She always likes to please people and I'll bet she changed her mind when she saw some senior management turn up."

"Well, we know who not to look to for help next time!" muttered Jim.

Describe the resulting problem

Previously the three had worked extremely well together. This was the beginning of a rift. Carol and Jim both started to notice faults

Your Notes

with Kathy and would point them out to each other. Pretty soon Kathy was on the outside.

Pose the following questions to the group

1. What do you see as the root of the problem?

   Likely responses:

   - Kathy didn't live up to her commitment.
   - There was no real agreement beforehand about what they would do.
   - Kathy was intimidated by management.

   Then add:

   Let me share with you some more information. Just before the meeting, Kathy received word that her father was critically ill. She had booked a flight home and rushed to the airport right after the meeting.

   Then ask, "Does this change the picture?"

2. What could have been done differently?

   Likely responses:

   - Jim and Carol could have asked Kathy what happened.
   - Kathy could have let Jim and Carol know that she had a personal problem.

3. Continue by asking, "I would like each of you to challenge yourselves as to whether you may have at some time responded to an illusion rather than facts. Have you ever made assumptions or jumped to conclusions?"

4. Distribute Workout (Handout H5.1).

5. Review the instructions. Emphasize that some of the reflections may be personal and although everyone is welcome to share their observations in question 1, no one should feel pressured to.

6. Allow 25 minutes for the Workout.

7. Invite workshop groups and individuals to share their observations and recommendations.

8. If appropriate, invite the team to turn their recommendations into team agreements.

Your Notes

WORKOUT: THINGS ARE NOT ALWAYS AS THEY SEEM

TIME REQUIRED: 25 minutes

INSTRUCTIONS

1. Individually identify an instance when someone misunderstood your actions, or you misunderstood someone else's. **Or** identify an instance when you disapproved of or were disappointed by what someone else did. Challenge yourself to consider possible alternative explanations to the one that seemed obvious to you.

2. Share your examples to the extent you are comfortable.

3. As a group, identify what team members can do differently to better prevent misunderstanding.

4. Be prepared to share your ideas with the larger group.

GAME 6 | ICE FLOE ADVENTURE

OBJECTIVES

Any or all of the following:

■ **To have fun!**

■ **To test and develop team decision making and problem solving skills.**

TIME REQUIRED:

Approximately one hour depending on the size of the team.

OVERVIEW

This game works well outdoors, although it can be done indoors, providing there is plenty of space.

In this game participants become members of an adventure tour group that is camping in the Arctic. Most of the team members are stranded on an ice floe that is floating away from camp. The task is to get those team members off the floe and back to the camp. There are floating chunks of ice that can be used as stepping stones.

You will use long pieces of rope to create the edge of the original camp site and the edge of the ice floe. The piece of ice that has broken away should be about 20 feet from the main ice floe. You will use pieces of plastic (approximately three feet by three feet) or a board to represent chunks of ice that team members will use as stepping stones.

Separate the group into the two spaces, two members at the camp and the rest on the break away ice floe.

From *More Games Teams Play* by Leslie Bendaly © 2000, McGraw-Hill Ryerson.

> **Your Notes**

At the beginning of the game, your layout will look like this:

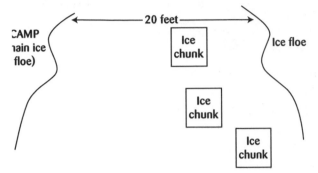

Note: If there are several participants (15 or more), you can have several groups completing this activity simultaneously. Then you can add a time element and competition—i.e. the group that gets all members across first wins.

MATERIALS REQUIRED

- Two pieces of rope—each approximately 10 feet long
- Three pieces of plastic or board—approximately three feet by three feet.

STEPS

1. Describe the scenario as follows:

Ice Floe Adventure

You are camping on an adventure tour in the Arctic. In early morning, while everyone was still in their tents, an ice floe broke away carrying most of your team members with it. Only two people are left at camp—the rest are floating away.

The only way for the group to get back is to cross the frigid water on chunks of ice dotted between the camp and the ice floe. The group must work together to find a way to get back to camp. The water is freezing. You must not get wet. If anyone falls off trying to get across, the whole group must go back and start over again.

2. Divide team as described in the Overview and position them on the two floes.

Your Notes

From *More Games Teams Play* by Leslie Bendaly © 2000, McGraw-Hill Ryerson.

3. Conduct the activity.

Note: Do not share the following information with participants unless they are stuck. Problem solving is an important part of this activity.

Once members begin the crossing, they will have to position a chunk of ice in front of them to move forward. Approximately three people can cross at one time. Once they have used all three chunks, they will have to move the last piece to the front of the line.

At least one person will have to go back to the floe after each trip to move the chunks back for others to cross.

4. Debrief.

Possible questions:

- You had to work together well in order to cross safely. What did you do well?
- Is there anything you could have done better?
- This was a difficult problem solving challenge. You were not seated comfortably around a meeting room table. What worked well? What didn't work well?
- How did those at the camp feel?

Usual response from those left at camp:

"Frustration because we couldn't actually do anything. They were all talking and excited and didn't listen to us."

- How did those on this ice floe feel?
- How do these experiences apply to your team back at work?

5. Recap key learnings.

Your Notes

GAME 7 | TEAM SLOGAN

OBJECTIVES

Any or all of the following:

- ■ **To increase team identity.**
- ■ **To increase awareness of the importance of the team "selling" itself within the organization.**
- ■ **To build team spirit.**

TIME REQUIRED: 1.5 hours

OVERVIEW

Increasing a team's sense of identity has a two-fold purpose. The greater the team sense of identity, the greater the team spirit and therefore the greater the team's energy. It is also essential that teams have a high and well-defined profile in their organization. Like individuals, teams must be seen to add value. Value is both real and perceived. The perceived value of the team, which will determine a team's success and longevity, is created by a combination of the results produced by the team and how it is seen in the organization. No one today, either team or individual can assume that their results "speak for themselves." The clearer teams are about their own identity and the greater their pride, the more likely they are to communicate that identity to others.

This activity challenges members to succinctly define and express what they have to offer by creating a slogan for the team. Recent examples of slogans from the market place include:

- "Time. The world's most interesting magazine."
- "IBM. Solutions for a small planet."
- "Brother. We're at your side."

> **Your Notes**

The team is not meant to necessarily use the slogan they create, although some do. The process of developing a slogan clarifies for the team what makes them unique. It may include what they have to offer but always emphasizes how they do what they do.

The subsequent discussion asks teams to consider whether the image suggested by the slogan is the one the team actually projects in the organization, and if not, what they need to do differently.

Your Notes

MATERIALS REQUIRED

- Enough copies of Handout (H7.1) for each team member.
- Sheets of paper (flip chart size).
- Coloured markers.
- Adhesive.

STEPS

1. The introduction is a presentation on the need for a high, positive and well-defined profile in the organization. You might use information from the overview above as well as evidence or examples from the team's organization.

2. If there are more than eight team members, break into smaller groups.

3. Distribute Handout H7.1 and review the instructions.

4. Conduct the activity and post the slogan(s).

5. Debrief.

   (a) Discuss the slogan(s).

   Possible Discussion Questions:
   - What does this slogan mean to you?
   - Do you believe your internal and/or external customers would recognize it as your slogan if your name weren't attached to it?
   - What can you do (more of or less of) to ensure the rest of the organization (and external customers) see you this way?

   (b) Invite commitment to the recommended actions the group identifies.

From *More Games Teams Play* by Leslie Bendaly © 2000, McGraw-Hill Ryerson.

CREATE YOUR TEAM'S SLOGAN

Your task is to create a slogan which creatively and succinctly describes the most important aspect(s) of what you as a team have to offer.

INSTRUCTIONS

1. As a group, list the team's key value points, i.e. what your team has to offer. Include both **what** you offer and **how** you do what you do.

KEY VALUE POINTS

What we offer	How we perform

2. Select from the list of Key Value Points two or three that are most important. Selection criteria might include:

   • They make you and your product or service unique or superior.

   • It is important that those who influence the team's resources and viability are aware of them.

3. Write a slogan that reflects your Key Value Points. Examples from the market place include:

   • "Time. The world's most interesting magazine."

   • "IBM. Solutions for a small planet."

   • "Brother. We're at your side."

   Be creative. Write your slogan in color with the materials provided.

GAME 8 IT PAYS TO ADVERTISE

OBJECTIVES

Any or all of the following:

- ▓ **To build the company team by getting to know one another better.**
- ▓ **To team build by working together on a creative task.**
- ▓ **To have fun!**

TIME REQUIRED: Three hours

OVERVIEW

Each team writes and produces a television commercial advertising the team itself. The completed commercial is videotaped and presented in front of the larger group. You may incorporate judging and prizes for the most creative and/or funniest videos.

It works well for the facilitator to show two or three popular or particularly funny television commercials at the beginning of the activity to help start the process.

ROOM SET-UP AND PLANNING

Ideally use breakout rooms so that each team can have quiet working space or a room large enough for teams to be spaced out. At least one breakout room is required to be used as the production studio—where the commercials will be videotaped. Depending on the number of teams, you may want more than one studio (and camera) so that videotaping can be done quickly and the momentum and energy are not lost.

TIP

Create a Production Studio sign for the door of the breakout room designated as the studio.

Your Notes

COACHES

Teams that are more creative by nature will get into the activity most quickly. Occasionally teams benefit from initial coaching. Assign coaches with creative ability and enthusiasm to circulate among the teams.

MATERIALS AND EQUIPMENT REQUIRED

- Handouts (H8.1 and H8.2).
- A video of two or three commercials, preferably humorous.
- Video camera(s) and videotapes.
- VCR and large screen/monitor (preferably giant screen).
- Colored paper, markers and adhesive for production studio sign(s).

PREPARATION

Consider the time lines presented on the Television Commercial Production Sheet (Handout H8.2). These represent the average time required by teams for each step. However, it is important that teams not be given too much time. You do not want to lose momentum. If you sense that the time lines are too long for your teams, tighten them up.

STEPS

1. Show the sample television commercials to get everyone's creative juices flowing.

2. Explain to the teams that now it is their turn to write and produce their own commercial advertising their team.

3. Distribute the It Pays to Advertise Briefing Sheet (Handout H8.1) and the Television Commercial Production Sheet (Handout H8.2).

4. Review the instructions. Emphasize that although some members may take roles such as lead writers, everyone is expected to contribute at each stage. At the writing stage for example, if the team is large, some members will act as a sounding board to ideas, or they may critique or

Your Notes

edit the script, etc. Roles do not have to be formally assigned, but full participation is essential.

5. Conduct the activity.

6. Screen the team commercials in front of the larger group.

7. If you decide to judge commercials and award prizes, you may:

   (a) Appoint judges (see Judge's Score Sheet, Handout H8.4).

   (b) Identify the winners by asking members of the audience to cheer for their preferred video. Ideally use an applause meter and stipulate that no team member may cheer for their own video. If you choose this option, show all videos once to allow a chance for comparison and then rerun them and invite applause and cheering for each.

8. A formal debriefing (optional) may be conducted which would explore teamwork within the individual teams during the production of the commercial:

   (a) Ask individual teams to work together to reflect on their experience by responding to the questions provided on the Advertising Teamwork Debriefing sheet (Handout H8.3).

   (b) Share and discuss responses to the questions.

   (c) Identify and recap learnings.

Your Notes

Handout
H8.1

IT PAYS TO ADVERTISE BRIEFING SHEET

Your task is to produce a television commercial that will sell your team as the best team "on the market." Be sure to include features and benefits. Features are characteristics; benefits are ways in which the product (your team) will meet the needs of the customer. For example, a real estate ad might read: "Spacious rooms" (feature). "Ideal for entertaining" (benefit).

Check your "Television Commercial Production Sheet" (Handout H8.2) for suggested time limits.

INSTRUCTIONS

1. Get organized. Clarify your task. Although all team members can participate in all aspects of the production, appoint lead writers, directors, camera people.

2. Brainstorm to identify team features and benefits and select those to be communicated in the commercial.

3. Brainstorm to identify a scenario.

4. Write the script.

5. Hold an audition for roles, and select actors.

6. Hold a rehearsal and make adjustments to the script.

7. Organize details, e.g. what costumes and sets are required and how best to improvise where necessary.

8. Produce your video.

TELEVISION COMMERCIAL PRODUCTION SHEET

Timetable	Task
15 minutes	Get organized/clarify task/assign roles.
40 minutes	Brainstorm to identify the team's features and benefits and select those to be communicated in the commercial.
30 minutes	Brainstorm to identify the best scenarios and select one.
45 minutes	Write the script. (**Do not rush.** Use the time allotted. Fine-tune if you are finished quickly.)
30 minutes	Hold an audition for the roles (or assign roles if your team members are reluctant actors). Hold a rehearsal and fine-tune the script.
20 minutes	Prepare for production. Determine what is needed for the set, etc.
15 minutes	Film your commercial (working in the production studio).

ADVERTISING TEAMWORK DEBRIEFING

1. How would you rate your teamwork in this activity? How well did you work together? Assign a score between 1 and 10, where 1 is poorly and 10 is very well.

   ☐ 1 ☐ 2 ☐ 3 ☐ 4 ☐ 5 ☐ 6 ☐ 7 ☐ 8 ☐ 9 ☐ 10

   Support your rating with specific examples of what you did very well or what you could have done better.

   _____

   _____

   _____

2. How did each member contribute to the process? Be specific.

   _____

   _____

   _____

3. If you were to do this again as a team, what would you do differently?

   _____

   _____

   _____

JUDGE'S SCORE SHEET

Rate each team's commercial with a score between 1 and 10 for each of the requirements, where 1 is a low score and 10 is a high score.

Commercial Requirements / Team Name	Team	Team	Team	Team	Team	Team
Presents the Team's Features						
Presents the Benefits the Team has to offer						
Shows Creativity						
Shows Humor						
Overall Quality						
TOTAL						

GAME 9 WHO DONE IT TO THE BOSS?

This game creates a fun and surprising kick-off at the beginning of your meeting, ensures a thread of fun is woven throughout the day and creates a high spirited wind-up.

Because it is company specific, it requires you to fill in the details.

OBJECTIVES

■ To have fun.

MATERIALS REQUIRED

- Video equipment.
- Handouts H9.1, H9.2, H9.3, H9.4, H9.5.

OVERVIEW

Attendees are challenged to find an article stolen from "the Boss" and to identify the thief.

The stolen article is something humorous—ideally something for which the boss is known or something that is a fond joke amongst staff.

Staff members are enlisted to play several roles. The senior manager should play himself or herself (the boss). One team member is required to play the thief and four others are needed as witnesses who have knowledge of the theft and/or where the article is hidden.

At the meeting, a kick-off video message from the boss is played on a giant screen. In the video the boss begins on a serious note (putting attendees just slightly on edge) and although he or she continues with a serious tone, the joke soon becomes evident. (See the Sample Script in Handout H9.1.)

The boss is usually a senior person who is not present. However, if he or she is present, the

Your Notes

individual introducing the video says something like "Jerry has something to say, but because of the emotional nature of the topic, he decided to tape his message."

The facilitator assigns all attendees to "Investigation" teams and briefs them. These teams may reflect operational teams or you may choose to create cross-functional teams for this game and perhaps assign a color to each team. The teams' challenge is to collect clues throughout the day and to identify the thief and the hiding place by the end of the meeting. Team members may or may not be together in an intact team throughout the day depending on your event's agenda. They will regroup three times for 15 minutes each time, at assigned times during the day to compare notes. Team members will have gathered information by questioning the staff members who have been identified as witnesses and from other clues that appear throughout the day.

At the end of the day, teams each announce their prime suspect and where they believe the loot was hidden. The real suspect gets up, admits his or her guilt and shows a slide of the object in its hiding place. The fun at this stage is increased when the object and hiding place are somehow related to "in" company jokes and personalities.

PREPARATION

1. Develop the scenario. What will be stolen? Who will steal it? Why did they steal it? (optional) Where did they hide it?

2. Make a game design decision. There are two options as to how teams can interrogate witnesses.

   (a) If the meeting/conference has 100 or less attendees, it can work well to have members "corner" the witnesses between sessions over lunch or coffee etc. Team members must then search out the witness. (Use the Investigation Team Briefing A, Handout H9.2.)

Your Notes

From *More Games Teams Play* by Leslie Bendaly © 2000, McGraw-Hill Ryerson.

(b) If however the conference/meeting is larger, structure the interrogations by setting up a 15 minute period during which a witness will meet with each team. The team can interrogate the witness for seven minutes of that time. Members may also question other witnesses should they bump into them during the day. (Investigation Team Briefing B, Handout H9.3) *Note:* There are also two briefings for witnesses, A and B, on Handout H9.5.

3. Assign roles and provide briefings. You must invite people to assume each role and explain their role to them.

   - The "boss" (Handout H9.1).
   - The thief (Handout H9.4). The thief may be a member of an Investigation Team.
   - Witnesses—four individuals with knowledge about the theft (number of witnesses depends on the number of attendees). If you have more than 60 in attendance, increase the number of witnesses. Determine which witness saw what. Some have knowledge of the theft, others of the hiding place, or both.

     If the conference is large and not everyone will know the individuals who play the witnesses, have them wear something to identify them, a t-shirt, arm band, etc.

   - Brief the witnesses together, if possible, so that everyone understands who knows what (Handout H9.5).

4. Tape the boss' message.

5. Develop clues and identify ways to communicate them or where to put them, e.g. in participants' package of conference meeting materials; notes in bread baskets on lunch tables; stuck on message board or walls.

6. Prepare and plant clues.

   Check with teams toward the end of the meeting to see whether anyone has

Your Notes

identified the thief or hiding place. *Don't let them know if they are right.* If no one has the answers, find a way to start dropping slightly

TIP

Start with subtle clues and build gradually through the day.

more obvious clues. However, don't give the answers away. You don't want every team to have the answer.

STEPS

1. Introduce and play the boss' video.

2. Assign investigations teams. Teams may be made up of members of intact/operational groups or you may decide to organize cross-functional teams for this activity and perhaps assign a color to each team.

3. Distribute Investigation Team Briefing sheets A (H9.2) or B (H9.3)—H9.2 is for smaller groups and H9.3 is for larger groups—over 100 attendees.

4. If using Briefing sheet B, ensure that the witnesses arrive at the right meeting room at the assigned time.

5. Provide clues throughout the day.

6. Check on teams' progress at approximately the three-quarter mark. If no one is close to identifying the thief and/or the hiding place, add more obvious clues.

7. At the end of the meeting, invite teams to each offer their solution, i.e. who did it and where is the loot hidden?

8. Reveal the thief.

9. The thief admits his/her guilt and reveals the hiding place.

10. Congratulate the winners.

Your Notes

From *More Games Teams Play* by Leslie Bendaly © 2000, McGraw-Hill Ryerson.

SAMPLE SCRIPT FOR THE BOSS

"Good morning.

"I hate to put a damper on your important meeting, however, I have something very serious that I felt I had to share with you quickly and wanted to ensure that you all received the news at the same time. **(pause for effect)**

"I discovered yesterday, to my great horror and disappointment, that there is a thief in our midst. As disturbing as this is for all of us at (name of organization), it must be faced. I have irrefutable evidence that my (name of item), a very cherished possession, has gone missing.

"I ask you to help me find the person who committed this dastardly deed and to find my (item) and return it safely to me.

"There will be two generous rewards: one for the team that can return my (item) undamaged to me and one for the team who identifies the culprit in our midst.

"Once again, I'm sorry to have to bring this unfortunate incident up during this important event and wish you a very good day."

From *More Games Teams Play* by Leslie Bendaly © 2000, McGraw-Hill Ryerson.

INVESTIGATION TEAM BRIEFING—A

Your task is to identify the thief and find the hiding place of the stolen goods by the end of our meeting.

You may approach any of the witnesses for information throughout the day. You may only ask two questions at any one time. You must ask questions that can be answered by a yes or no. You may **not** suggest a name and question anyone as to whether that person is the guilty party, e.g. Did Tom do it?

You have 15 minutes to get organized and your team will regroup for 15 minutes, three times during the day to share the information gathered and discuss possible suspects and hiding places.

Stay alert for other clues that may come your way.

Have fun!

INVESTIGATION TEAM BRIEFING—B

Your task is to identify the thief and find the hiding place for the stolen goods by the end of our meeting.

You have 10 minutes now to get organized. You will regroup in 15 minute meetings three times during the day. In your first meeting, a witness will visit you. You may interrogate them for seven minutes, but you must only ask questions that can be answered by a yes or no. You may **not** ask whether a specific staff member is guilty, e.g. Did Tom do it?

You may question other witnesses if you bump into them during the day. **Watch for other clues in unexpected places.**

Have fun!

THIEF BRIEFING

Your role is to simply act as you normally would. Do not let any information slip that might incriminate you. You may be a member of an Investigation Team.

At the end, on the pre-determined signal from the organizer, stand up, come to center stage, act guilty and remorseful. Show the slide of the object in its hiding place (provided by facilitator). Destroy these instructions once you understand!

WITNESS BRIEFING

SCENARIO A

You have been a witness to the crime. You have knowledge along with the facilitator of either who did it or where the object is hidden or both.

Ensure you clarify with the facilitator what knowledge you are to have.

You will be approached by members of the Investigation Teams and asked questions that you can answer **only** by responding yes or no.

An individual can ask you only two questions at one time. Be careful not to give clues with your body language or facial expressions.

SCENARIO B

In addition to the above, you will meet with at least one Investigation Team. They may ask you questions for seven minutes which you can answer **only** by responding yes or no. Please check your watch at the beginning and leave promptly after seven minutes.

GAME 10   LIVING BY THE LAW OF PURPOSE AND PASSION

OBJECTIVES

One or all of the following:

- ■ **To understand the importance of working with purpose and passion.**
- ■ **To test the degree to which the team works with purpose and passion.**
- ■ **To increase the degree to which the team works with purpose and passion.**

TIME REQUIRED: one hour

OVERVIEW

Psychologist Ernest Becker once said, "It's not that man so much fears death but death with insignificance."

More people are looking for more than just money for the hours they spend working. They want to feel they have made a contribution. The clearer the team's purpose and the greater its passion in fulfilling it, the more fulfilled its members will be. And subsequently, the more energized and successful the team.

Too many are burning out—they are using more energy than they are creating.

Constant change and heavy workloads burn excessive amounts of energy. When teams are excited about what they do, when they have purpose and passion, extra work and constant change are not such burdens. In this case more energy is created than what is expended. The following activity begins with word scramble games. One is designed as a task. The second is designed as a task with a purpose. The games lead into a discussion of this purpose. The remainder of the exercise challenges the team to develop a clear picture of its purpose and to examine and increase its passion.

Your Notes

Note: Should this team be mandated to accomplish something with which they are not in agreement, or for which they cannot generate excitement (something unpleasant such as making downsizing decisions, or a task that management sees as important but the team does not), *DO NOT USE* this exercise.

MATERIALS REQUIRED

- Handouts.
- Two prizes.
- Box large enough to hold prizes.
- Red paper to cover box or marker to color it red.
- Several other colored markers.
- Adhesive.
- Two sheets of bristol board or other heavy paper.

PREPARATION

1. Purchase two team prizes, i.e. several small prizes (one for each person in each of two teams) or a prize that can be shared.

2. Prepare the box. Cover it with red paper or color it red with a colored marker. Before the session begins, set it in a corner at the front end of the room or with the workshop supplies.

3. Write "Our Purpose" in large letters on a piece of bristol board (see page 138).

4. On the second piece of bristol board, write the heading "Passion Barometer" and draw a barometer below the heading (see page 139).

STEPS

1. Introduction.

   (a) Ask participants to complete the word scramble (Handout H10.1).

   (b) Check answers, celebrate success.

   Answers to Handout H10.1:

   toenail
   carton
   veranda

Your Notes

parachute
river
doorstep
circus

(c) Explain that you will now ask them to complete a similar but different task. Tell the group that you have hidden two prizes in the room. They can find the prizes by unscrambling another set of scrambled words (Handout H10.2) and using the circled letters to spell out the location of the hidden prize.

(d) Ask the participants to complete the activity. The group will solve the puzzle and find the prizes in the red box.

Answers to Handout H10.2:

1. recent
2. easy
3. double
4. build
5. otter
6. relax

The first letters of the answers to Questions 1 to 5 plus the last letter of the answer to Question 6 spell: red box.

(e) Debrief.

Possible question:
What was the difference between the first and second word scramble activities?

Likely responses:
The first was fun, but the second had a purpose.

Possible question:
How does this apply to your team?

You may continue with a mini presentation described below or skip to Step 3.

Give a brief presentation on how purpose and passion have energized people and groups to endure and succeed in spite of enormous obstacles and/or how the lack of passion has hindered success.

Your Notes

Examples from History:

- Britain's determination and spirit in spite of the repeated bombing of London is an inspiring example of passion. "We can't say we're doing our best. We have to do what has to be done!" *Winston Churchill*

  Purpose and passion allowed the British to do more than their best.

- Lack of belief in the Vietnam War and how that affected the war experience and the outcome is a good example of the impact of lack of purpose and passion.

Individual Achievement:

- Lance Armstrong won the Tour de France bicycle race in 1999 after recovering from cancer.

  A sense of purpose can create passion.

3. Post the "Our Purpose" bristol board on a wall or large board.

4. Ask each team member to write a short sentence describing the team purpose. Ask them to use the markers and paper provided and write large enough to fill the entire sheet.

5. Ask participants to post their descriptions on the wall around the "Our Purpose" title. Here is what your Purpose board might look like at this stage:

Your Notes

From *More Games Teams Play* by Leslie Bendaly © 2000, McGraw-Hill Ryerson.

6. Compare and discuss the descriptions of the team purpose. Look for commonalities. Remove the statements for which there is not agreement.

7. Post a statement of purpose developed from the discussion.

8. Ask each member to rate the degree of passion that the team demonstrates for its purpose (on a 1 to 10 scale where 1 is a low score and 10 is a high score).

9. Collect the responses and determine the average degree of passion.

10. Post the Passion Barometer bristol board beside the purpose statement and mark the team's degree of passion. At this stage, the wall or large board will look like this:

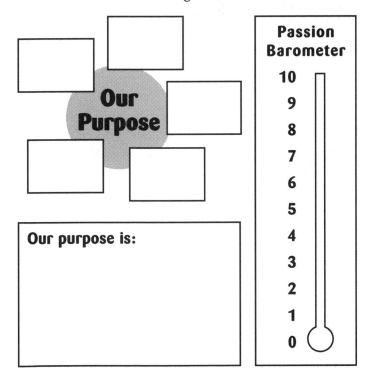

11. Ask the team members what they can do to increase the team's passion. If time allows, this can be discussed in smaller groups and then invite each group to share two or three recommendations with the larger group.

12. Discuss the recommendations. Identify those seen as the most important to the group.

Your Notes

13. Recap the recommendations and invite the group to commit to working on them. Put a follow-up system in place so that the team can check whether it is living up to the agreement.

Your Notes

WORD SCRAMBLE I

Unscramble each of the following words:

l e o a n i t   _ _ _ _ _ _ _

t n o r a c   _ _ _ _ _ _

d n r a v e a   _ _ _ _ _ _ _

e h c r a a p t u   _ _ _ _ _ _ _ _ _

v r e r i   _ _ _ _ _

d p s e o t r o   _ _ _ _ _ _ _ _

c c s r u i   _ _ _ _ _ _

Handout
H10.2

WORD SCRAMBLE II

Unscramble the following words to find where two prizes have been hidden. As soon as you get the answer, quickly run to get a prize from the hidden location. Remember there are only two prizes!

The first letters of each unscrambled word in Questions 1 to 5 plus the last letter of the answer to Question 6 will spell out the hiding place.

1. c r e e t n ◯ _ _ _ _ _

2. y s a e ◯ _ _ _

3. l o u e b d ◯ _ _ _ _ _

4. d u i b l ◯ _ _ _ _

5. r e t t o ◯ _ _ _ _

6. x l a r e _ _ _ _ ◯

Answer: _ _ _ _ _ _

GAME 11 "I KNOW WHAT YOU DID LAST NIGHT"

A fun, getting to know you, energizer, which works well after a lunch break.

OBJECTIVES

One or all of the following:

- **To get to know one another.**
- **To check how well team members know one another.**
- **To have fun.**

TIME REQUIRED: Approximately 20 minutes

MATERIALS REQUIRED

- Pens and paper.

OVERVIEW

Each team member writes on a piece of paper something that he or she did the evening before. The leader reads them out and team members try to guess who did what.

STEPS

1. Ask team members to each write something they did the evening before using the pens and the paper provided (so all responses look alike) and give it to you. Remind them not to write something that they have already shared with any members.

2. During a break, organize the pieces of information by arbitrarily numbering each one.

3. Read each piece of information aloud along with its number. Ask participants to write down the number and the person they think is the owner.

Your Notes

4. Re-read each piece of information, this time asking team members to call out the name of the person they think is the owner.

5. Ask the real owner to "please stand up."

6. Ask participants to tally their scores (one point for each correct guess) and share the top results.

Your Notes

GAME 12 | THE CABIN IN THE WOODS

OBJECTIVE

■ To remind members to go beyond the obvious solution and check assumptions.

TIME REQUIRED: One-half hour

MATERIALS REQUIRED

- Overhead T12.1.

BACKGROUND

People often complain that problem solving and decision making take too long. Often the opposite is true. Teams frequently jump to a conclusion without recognizing and challenging their assumptions.

This activity can stand on its own to heighten a team's awareness of assumptions or can be used before an important problem solving or decision making exercise.

STEPS

1. Introduce the activity by telling the team that you are going to ask them to solve a problem. Break a larger group into smaller groups of six to eight people (ideally).

2. Explain that you are going to give each group an identical problem to solve and their task is to try to be the first group to solve it.

3. Explain the following rules:

   (a) One member from each team will be given the answer to the problem which is in the form of a riddle.

   (b) The facilitator will share the riddle with everyone (on overhead, flipchart or by distributing copies to each group).

Your Notes

(c) Teams must try to get the answer by asking questions that can be answered only by a yes or no. Should a question be asked in a form that cannot be answered by a yes or no, it must be reworded.

(d) The first group to guess the correct solution wins.

4. Share the right answer with one member from each group. (Either give each representative the answer in an envelope or take the representatives outside together and share the answer verbally. The benefit of the second method is that the facilitator can then check the group's understanding of the rules and the solution with the representatives.)

Answer: The cabin is the cabin of a plane that has crashed in the woods.

5. Share the riddle (T12.1) and conduct the activity.

6. Congratulate the winners.

7. Conduct a debriefing.

(a) Possible Discussion Question:

What factors were important to your being able to discover what happened?

Likely responses:

- "Checking our assumptions—when we heard 'cabin in the woods,' we immediately thought of a log cabin."
  OR
- "Looking at alternatives before we forged down one path. No one questioned our initial response—we all went in the same direction."

(b) Recap the key points.

Include:

- Our personal experience or frame of reference can cause us to make assumptions. If we all have the same experience, we are likely to make the same assumption, or all work within the same paradigm.

Your Notes

- Members who bring different experiences to the group can bring a different and valuable perspective. Sometimes because they are in a minority position, their points of view may not be heard or they may be hesitant to voice them.

(c) Application Options:

- Can you identify past problem solving experiences when assumptions decreased the effectiveness of your outcomes?
  AND/OR
- What might the team agree to do to prevent assumptions from negatively influencing the quality of your problem solving processes?

Your Notes

THE CABIN IN THE WOODS

You have come across a cabin in the woods. Inside are many dead people. They are seated in rows of chairs. What happened?

From *More Games Teams Play* by Leslie Bendaly © 2000, McGraw-Hill Ryerson.

GAME 13 MAKES ME THINK OF...

OBJECTIVES

Any or all of the following:

■ **To increase the understanding of the different life experiences team members bring to a team experience.**

■ **To increase the effectiveness of our communication.**

TIME REQUIRED: One hour

MATERIALS REQUIRED

- Handouts H13.1 and H13.2.

BACKGROUND

Team communication frequently breaks down because members assume a common understanding. Members may have certain expectations of a team member based on the assumption that a team member sees an issue as they do.

Even among people with common backgrounds, perceptions of shared events, experiences, even words vary greatly. In a diverse society, these different views are compounded.

This activity illustrates how even common concepts or words mean different things to different members.

STEPS

1. Distribute the Worksheet, Handout H13.1.

2. Review the instructions.

3. Conduct the individual activity (10 minutes).

4. Distribute the Team Scoring Sheets, Handout H13.2.

Your Notes

5. Compare scores.

6. Discuss the outcomes.

Possible Discussion Question:
What surprised you about the outcome?

Likely response:
"We had no (or almost no) responses in common. You would assume that a simple word like 'family' would mean similar things to everyone."

7. Sum up the learning, perhaps using points mentioned in the Background section.

8. Discuss the various applications of the learning.

Discussion Questions:

- How does the learning from this activity apply to your teamwork?
- What can each of you as team members do to prevent misunderstanding or unrealistic expectations?

Likely responses:

- "We need to check for understanding."
- "We should better explain what we expect rather than assuming others will behave in a certain way."

When appropriate, draw specific examples from the team.

9. Invite the team to commit to recommendations that everyone supports.

Your Notes

WORKSHEET

Write down every word that comes to mind when you think of the word "family." Please work quietly and independently. Don't share the words you think of with others.

_____   _____   _____

_____   _____   _____

_____   _____

_____   **Family**   _____

_____   _____

_____   _____   _____

TEAM SCORING SHEET

INSTRUCTIONS

Check the words you associate with "family" with those identified by your team members.

Give yourself a point for each word that every team member had on their worksheet. Words must be identical. Mom and mother, for example, are not the same words.

Total score: _____

GAME 14 GETTING THE POINT

OBJECTIVE

■ **To develop team members' awareness of the importance of dialogue and the requirements for achieving it.**

TIME REQUIRED: 40 minutes

BACKGROUND

Frequently, in team discussions, members focus on communicating their own ideas or "selling" their point of view. *In dialogue, members have a dual responsibility: to present their own ideas effectively; and to actively make an effort to understand others' perspectives.* In effective dialogue, members make an effort to prove others "right."

This workout puts members in the position of having to focus on their own point of view to dramatize the fact that this behavior is common in meetings. People are so busy focusing on their idea that they often don't listen to or try to understand those of others. Dialogue is then impossible and team members do not connect powerfully enough to create synergy.

MATERIALS REQUIRED

• Handouts H14.1 and H14.2, Overhead T14.1.

PREPARATION

Identify two or three controversial topics that team members might discuss.

STEPS

1. Explain to the group that you are going to ask them to apply their team skills to try to come to a consensus on a "hot" issue.

Your Notes

2. Present the group with the issue or allow them to choose one of two or three options.

3. Distribute and review the instructions (Handout H14.1) for the workout.

4. Conduct the workout (allow 20 minutes).

5. Ask whether everyone made their four points. Most will respond yes. Then say "Now what I want you to do is to make a list of all the points made by each of your team mates." You are likely to get laughter and groans.

6. Let participants work long enough on their lists to get a sense of the difficulty most will have in remembering others' points.

7. You might say "This workout was called "Getting the Point." What is the point we can get from the workout?"

   Possible response:
   "We are usually so busy making our own points that we don't really listen to others."

8. Make a short presentation on dialogue using information from Background and Overhead T14.1. Distribute Handout H14.2.

9. Ask: "What can you do to improve dialogue within your team?"

10. Recap points that the group has agreed on and ask for commitment to them.

Your Notes

From *More Games Teams Play* by Leslie Bendaly © 2000, McGraw-Hill Ryerson.

GETTING THE POINT— INSTRUCTIONS

TIME REQUIRED: 20 minutes

1. Select a discussion topic if one has not already been assigned by your facilitator.

2. Decide who will take for and against positions.

3. Individually jot down four points to support your position on the topic.

4. Each group member is responsible for ensuring that they present each of their four points in the discussion even if someone else has made the same point(s).

5. Try to come to agreement.

CONNECTING THROUGH DIALOGUE

Connecting is essential.

Connecting only works when it is two-way.

Connecting requires dialogue: Meeting members must recognize the difference between discussion and dialogue.

In dialogue, there is a dual responsibility:

- To understand others' points of view.
- To communicate their own points effectively.

Dialogue is essential to:

- Personal growth (learning) and the shifting of personal paradigms.
- The best decisions and outcomes.

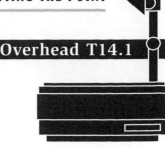

DIALOGUE

In dialogue, members have a dual responsibility:

- to actively make an effort to understand others' perspectives; and

- to present their own ideas effectively.

GAME 15 FEELIN' GOOD

OBJECTIVES

One or all of the following:

- **To improve the team's climate.**
- **To encourage members to make a conscious effort to help others feel good about themselves.**

TIME REQUIRED: 45 minutes

BACKGROUND

Energy depletion is a serious concern in the workplace. Burnout is a common problem as workloads increase. One statistic suggested that the average worker in the United States in 1998 worked one month per year more than in 1970. Canadians stand third in the world for most hours worked per year. However, the main reason for energy depletion is not due to workload, but instead to negative feelings about the work and/or workplace. Hans Selye, often referred to as the father of stress management, insisted that work didn't cause stress as long people were happy performing it.

Energy is one essential resource that cannot be purchased from a supplier. It must be created from within. When people feel good about themselves, the team energy supply is increased.

Frequently, because team members are busy, insensitive or simply careless, they miss opportunities to help others feel good about themselves.

You are provided with two activities. Choose the one you feel would best work with the group you have in mind.

Your Notes

VERSION I

MATERIALS REQUIRED

- Handouts (either H15.1 or H15.2).

STEPS

1. Introduce the workshop by using the information provided in Background.

2. Organize participants into discussion groups of six to eight people.

3. Distribute Handout H15.1 and review the instructions.

4. Conduct the activity.

5. Invite discussion teams to share their ideas with the larger group.

6. Lead the group in selecting the five or six key ideas that they believe to be most important.

7. Invite the group to commit to following through on them in the workplace.

VERSION II

MATERIALS REQUIRED

- Large sheets of bristol board.
- Colored construction paper.
- Colored markers.
- Adhesive, e.g. stickum gum.

PREPARATION

Prepare a "Feelin' Good" heading on a sheet of bristol board. If the group contains more than seven or eight team members, use an oversized sheet or put several boards together.

STEPS

1. For the presentation and introduction, you may use information from the Background. You may also want to include something like "Individuals have different needs. What makes some feel good may not be important to you. It may even make you uncomfortable. For example, some people

Your Notes

enjoy personal recognition programs such as 'employee of the month.' Others find them embarrassing."

2. Ask participants to write on their colored paper one thing that team members can do that makes them feel particularly good. Examples might include:

   - "Others can compliment me on a job well done."
   - "People can ask if they can help me."
   - "Others can share information with me."
   - "People can ask for my advice."

3. Ask participants to sign their statement and stick it on the board.

4. Invite participants to review the statements and add their name to those which also apply to them.

5. Discuss the results. Note for example, any statements that have only one or two names on them and make the observation that "since (this item) is important only to (member's name) and (member's name), the rest of you might not think to give these members something that is important to them." You might ask: "To what extent do you do these things now? Which behaviors require more attention?"

6. Invite the team to commit to making a conscious effort to make others feel good about themselves.

Your Notes

FEELIN' GOOD!!

The amount of energy created by a team is directly related to how the team members feel about themselves. People who feel good about themselves produce positive energy. People who feel badly about themselves not only do not create energy but they can also deplete the team's energy store.

Team members contribute greatly to how other members feel about themselves.

In your team:

1. Identify what the team/team members can do to help ensure that all team members feel good about themselves. List the suggestions on a piece of paper.

2. Examine the list you have created and for each item, rate how well you do that now. (Use a rating scale from 1 to 4 where 1 is poorly and 4 represents very well/all of the time.)

3. Identify:

   (a) What you should do more of.

   (b) What you should do less of.

4. Be prepared to share three ideas with the larger group.

GAME 16 A SCAVENGER HUNT FOR THE EYES

OBJECTIVES

Any or all of the following:

- ▓ **To demonstrate teamwork.**
- ▓ **To build the team.**
- ▓ **To have fun!**

TIME REQUIRED: One hour (approximately)

BACKGROUND

This game is a twist on the traditional scavenger hunt. Teams are given a map that indicates the scavenger hunt route.

The hunt takes place on the conference site or in an area close to it. It may be a country or city setting. Teams are given the map with a set of riddles created by the facilitator. They follow the route and solve the riddles by identifying objects or places along the route. Here are a few examples from a conference that was held in a city setting:

Riddle	Object to Be Identified
1. Look up high and you will find A brand you know in the center of time.	A clock with a beer ad on its face over a store door.
2. The spot where the rich and famous and the rest Come to look their very best.	A well known spa.
3. A spot to stay if you dare to enter.	Venture Inn.
4. Spring, summer, winter, fall. He opens the door for them all. (What is his name?)	The name of the doorman at the Four Seasons Hotel.

The facilitator must of course visit the site in advance and create a set of riddles. Creative facilitators enjoy this preparation and teams always have fun with it.

PREPARATION

1. Scout the site for a location.

2. Jot down names of buildings, places, spots, etc. to use in the riddles (e.g. see Background examples).

3. Write rhymes to represent each allowing space on the sheet to enter their responses.

4. Draw the map indicating a route or the parametres of the Scavenger area. (If at a resort setting, you might not use a map but just send the group outdoors to search.)

MATERIALS REQUIRED

- Maps.
- Set of riddles.
- Handouts.
- Prizes.

STEPS

1. Introduce the game and distribute Handout H16.1.

2. Break group into teams (preferably five to eight people so that they can work together well). Hand out maps and riddles to each group. If you are working with a very large group, ensure each team receives several copies of the maps and riddles so that everyone can participate easily.

3. Give teams an allotted time based on the size of the area to be covered.

4. When the groups return, energetically check responses. Congratulate the winner(s), i.e. the group(s) with the highest scores.

5. Optional—Allow time for a Team Debrief. Distribute Debriefing Handout H16.2. Allow teams 15 to 30 minutes to complete it, depending on the depth of discussion you wish to encourage.

Your Notes

RULES FOR THE SCAVENGER HUNT

1. To qualify to win, all members must stay together at all times.

2. Teams receive two points for each correct answer.

3. The team that finishes first receives two bonus points.

4. The team with the highest point score wins.

DEBRIEF THE SCAVENGER HUNT

As a group, consider how your team worked together in the Scavenger Hunt.

1. Appoint a discussion leader.

2. Identify the various skills and aptitudes team members brought to the activity, e.g. Did someone take a leadership role? Was someone an organizer? Were some people particularly good at solving the riddles? etc.

(continued)

Team Member's Name	Skill/Aptitude

3. As a team, what did you do well that contributed to your success? For example, did you ensure everyone was included? Did you build on each other's ideas? Did you develop a plan of action?

4. How could you have worked more effectively as a team?

GAME 17 SAY IT IN PICTURES

OBJECTIVES

Any or all of the following:

- **To reinforce an important meeting/ conference theme; corporate or team values; corporate or team mission statement.**
- **To team build.**

TIME REQUIRED: 2.5 hours (approximately)

MATERIALS REQUIRED

- Polaroid camera and film for each team.
- Large sheets of bristol board for mounting pictures (one per team).
- Paper, pens, adhesive, colored markers.
- Prizes (optional).
- Handout H17.1.

BACKGROUND

This is a fun team building activity that reinforces key concepts or themes such as team values or mission statements. It draws on team skills, members' observation skills, creativity and often humor.

The larger group is divided into manageable sized teams (preferably under 10 to encourage full participation). Each team is provided with a Polaroid camera and assigned the task of developing a collage of photos that expresses the... (values, mission statement, etc.). Each team is asked to present their collage to the larger group. Each photo collage is judged and prizes awarded (optional).

PREPARATION

1. Identify the theme that the pictures illustrate and your expectations, e.g.:
   - One photo to represent each team or corporate value.

Your Notes

- Several photos which represent the corporate or team mission statement.
- Photos that represent the theme of your meeting or conference.

2. Purchase and organize materials.

3. Decide whether the collages will be judged and if so, using which of the judging methods described below. *Note:* The handout provided (H17.1) includes a reference to judging. If you eliminate judging, you will need to prepare a new set of instructions.

   (a) Teams may judge one another. In this method, provide each team with a Judging Sheet (Handout H17.2) and ask them to rate each collage *except* their own. They must come to consensus on the rating which is in itself another team building exercise. Teams then submit the completed sheets. Organizers tally the totals on the sheets and announce the winners based on the averages.

   (b) Appoint judges (anyone not part of the activity, i.e. guests, organizers, etc.) to decide which team's collage best meets the requirements described (H17.2).

STEPS

1. You might provide an introduction describing the team skills required to successfully complete the activity including creativity, collaboration and consensus reaching.

2. Distribute the Say It In Pictures Instructions sheet (Handout H17.1) and material and review instructions with the group.

3. Conduct the activity.

4. Invite each team to present its collage.

5. Judge the collages. (Judges or judging teams may need more than one Judging Sheet (Handout H17.2), depending on number of teams.)

6. Award prizes (optional). Celebrate everyone's contribution.

Your Notes

From *More Games Teams Play* by Leslie Bendaly © 2000, McGraw-Hill Ryerson.

SAY IT IN PICTURES— INSTRUCTIONS

1. Your task is to create a collage of pictures that represents…

2. You have two hours to create a team name, find your photo subjects, take your pictures and organize them, select a presenter or presenters and develop your presentation. **Tip:** Scout for photo subjects first and list them. Decide as a team on the best choices and then snap them. Remember you have only one film!

3. You must stay together as a team throughout the whole process. Full participation is required!

4. You will be judged on each of the following:
   - Creativity of team name chosen.
   - Creativity in subjects chosen.
   - Visual presentation of collage.
   - Creativity of presentation content.
   - Delivery of presentation.
   - Humor and elements of fun.

5. Your kit should include:
   - One sheet of bristol board.
   - One Polaroid camera and film.
   - Paper, pens, adhesive, colored markers.

6. Create a team name and put it on your collage.

Have fun!

SAY IT IN PICTURES— JUDGING SHEET

TEAM NAME OR NUMBER:

Rate each requirement on a 1 to 5 scale, where 1 is a low score and 5 is a high score, by circling your selection.

Requirements					
Creativity of team name	1	2	3	4	5
Creativity in subjects chosen	1	2	3	4	5
Visual presentation of collage	1	2	3	4	5
Creativity of presentation content	1	2	3	4	5
Delivery of presentation	1	2	3	4	5
Humor and elements of fun	1	2	3	4	5
TOTAL					

GAME 18
ACCORDING TO... –REPEAT PERFORMANCE

We introduced "According to..." in the original *Games Teams Play*. In response to the positive feedback we have had on this activity, we are providing it again with new quotes that we have found act as good catalysts for a team building activity.

OBJECTIVE

■ **To encourage creative thinking about how the team works and to identify opportunities for improvement.**

TIME REQUIRED: 30 minutes +

BACKGROUND

Teams that thrive do not take their success for granted. They recognize that success is due not only to what they do but to how the team functions.

This activity challenges members to escape vertical thinking patterns and explore aspects of the team's performance that normally would not be considered.

Team members will be provided with a selection of quotations that will act as a catalyst for team members' thinking. The quotations are varied and will trigger different thoughts in different members. *Note:* You have several sets of quotations from which to choose.

MATERIALS REQUIRED

- Overheads and Handouts (choose one set):
  - Set 1 (corresponding with Handout H18.1), T18.1 and T18.2
  - Set 2 (corresponding with Handout H18.2), T18.3 and T18.4

Your Notes

STEPS

1. Present the quotations to the group using the overhead for the set of quotations selected.

2. Select one quotation and lead an introductory discussion.

   Possible question:
   Does this quotation trigger any thoughts about your team?

   This mini discussion is meant to focus the group and to "prime the well" for the individual thinking that follows.

3. Provide each participant with the corresponding copy of the "According to..." worksheet (Handout H18.1 *or* H18.2). Briefly review the instructions. Allow approximately 10 minutes for completion of the worksheet.

   Variation—Invite participants to complete the worksheets in small groups. Select or ask the group to select three or four quotations. Allow approximately 25 minutes.

4. Discuss each quotation, asking participants to share their responses.

5. Recap observations and any opportunities for improvement that evolve from this discussion.

6. Lead the group in identifying which opportunities for improvement can be turned into commitments to action.

7. Check for consensus.

   Outcomes

   - Better understanding of one another's perspectives.
   - New perspectives on how the team works.
   - Commitments to action that will increase team effectiveness.

Your Notes

THOUGHTS FOR TEAMS

"Management of the team process must become part of the task."

Leslie Bendaly
Author and Corporate Coach

"The man who never alters his opinion is like standing water, and breeds reptiles of the mind."

William Blake, 1757–1827
English Poet and Artist

[Referring to the changing times]
"A great wind is blowing, and that gives you either imagination or a headache."

Catherine II ("The Great")
Empress of Russia

THOUGHTS FOR TEAMS

"Panta rei—all is flux...
[Therefore] you cannot step
twice into the same river."

Heraclitus
Greek Philosopher

"Change is the law of life.
And those who look only to the
past or present are certain to
miss the future."

John F. Kennedy
Former U.S. President

THOUGHTS FOR TEAMS

"I never discovered anything with my rational mind."

Albert Einstein
Scientist, Inventor

"Imagination is the main source of value in the new economy."

Tom Peters
Author and Management Guru

"The task of the leader is to get his people from where they are to where they have not been."

Henry Kissinger
Former U.S. Secretary of State

THOUGHTS FOR TEAMS

"Doing the little things right in every play makes the difference between winning and losing."

Michael "Pinball" Clemons
Football Player

"We cannot succeed if we are going against our nature. We cannot fail if we are true to ourselves."

Author Unknown

ACCORDING TO— WORKSHEET

Quotation	Thoughts About Your Team
"Management of the team process must become part of the task." Leslie Bendaly Author and Corporate Coach	
"The man who never alters his opinion is like standing water, and breeds reptiles of the mind." William Blake, 1757–1827 English Poet and Artist	
[Referring to the changing times] "A great wind is blowing, and that gives you either imagination or a headache." Catherine II ("The Great") Empress of Russia	
"*Panta rei*—all is flux...[Therefore] you cannot step twice into the same river." Heraclitus Greek Philosopher	
"Change is the law of life. And those who look only to the past or present are certain to miss the future." John F. Kennedy Former U.S. President	

From *More Games Teams Play* by Leslie Bendaly © 2000, McGraw-Hill Ryerson.

ACCORDING TO— WORKSHEET

Quotation	Thoughts About Your Team
"I never discovered anything with my rational mind." Albert Einstein Scientist, Inventor	
"Imagination is the main source of value in the new economy." Tom Peter Author and Management Guru	
"The task of the leader is to get his people from where they are to where they have not been." Henry Kissinger Former U.S. Secretary of State	
"Doing the little things right in every play makes the difference between winning and losing." Michael "Pinball" Clemons Football Player	
"We cannot succeed if we are going against our nature. We cannot fail if we are true to ourselves." Author Unknown	

GAME 19 TEAM TRIATHLON A

OBJECTIVES

One or all of the following:

- **To energize group members and have fun.**
- **To encourage the use of various strengths, e.g. verbal ability, numeric ability, visual problem solving, etc.**
- **To encourage creativity.**

TIME REQUIRED: 15 minutes

OVERVIEW

The "Team Triathlon" in the original *Games Teams Play* was so popular that other versions have been provided.

Each of the three challenges in a Team Triathlon requires a different skill set or aptitude. This variety stretches participants' minds in several directions and ensures that most, if not all participants will be able to contribute strongly in at least one of the challenges.

The rules for each triathlon are identical. The group is organized into teams of six to 10 members (ideally). Teams receive three envelopes, each containing a different challenge.

The game is competitive and teams win based on the number of correct answers and their speed (teams receive bonus points for finishing first).

On the signal from the facilitator, teams open the envelope marked Challenge #1. Once they have solved the problem, they send a runner to the facilitator with their answer. If it is correct, they move on to the envelope marked Challenge #2. If not, they must try again. (If several teams have moved on and one or two are stumped, you may suggest that they too move ahead. They will not receive the point for that activity.)

Your Notes

Once they have solved as many brain teasers as possible in the envelope marked Challenge #2, they move to Challenge #3. However, once they set an envelope aside, they can't return to it.

When they have completed Challenge #3, they signal that they are finished by singing a loud round of a simple song, e.g. *Three Blind Mice*.

SCORING

Teams receive one point for each correct answer, plus two points for finishing first—i.e. *beginning* to sing the song first.

MATERIALS REQUIRED

- Instructions (one sheet per participant).
- Three or four copies of each of the three challenges selected for each group.
- Three envelopes for each group.

PREPARATION

Copy The Team Triathlon—Instructions (Handout H19.1) and Challenges selected (H19.2, 3 and 4) and put challenges into envelopes. Number each envelope according to the number of the challenge inside, i.e., Challenge #1, etc.

STEPS

1. Distribute the instructions and envelopes.
2. Review the instructions with the group.
3. Conduct the game.

ANSWERS

Challenge #1—fast.

Challenge #2

1. The big picture.
2. Twin peaks.
3. Without a single cent.
4. Look backwards.
5. Account overdrawn.
6. Forlorn.
7. Eye shadow.
8. Hidden agenda.

Challenge #3—unscrambled words—plate, spoon, knife, bottle

Answer: bottle

Your Notes

THE TEAM TRIATHLON— INSTRUCTIONS

1. You will receive a set of three envelopes. Your task as a group is to complete each of the challenges presented in the envelopes as accurately and quickly as possible.

2. Wait until the leader signals to open Challenge #1. When you have an answer to the problem presented, assign a team member to check your answer with the leader. If you have the correct answer, go on to Challenge #2. If not try again.

3. Envelope #2 contains several brain teasers. Once you have solved as many brain teasers as possible, go on to Challenge #3. **Note: You may not return to an earlier challenge once you have set it aside.**

4. When you have solved the last challenge (Challenge #3), signal that you are finished by loudly singing a verse of _____ _____.

TEAM TRIATHLON A— CHALLENGE #1

Find what each of the following words has in common.

food

cars

friends

Common denominator:_____

Handout
H19.3

TEAM TRIATHLON A— CHALLENGE #2

Solve each of the following brain teasers by determining the phrase depicted.

1. **PICTURE**

2. PEAK PEAK

3. 2 cents
   3 cents
   4 cents
   5 cents

4. KOOL

5. account
   drawn

6. Lorn
   Lorn
   Lorn
   Lorn

7. **eye**

8. aghidenda

TEAM TRIATHLON A— CHALLENGE #3

Find the one that doesn't fit:

elpat

oposn

ekifn

lttboe

Answer: _____

GAME 20 TEAM TRIATHLON B

OBJECTIVES

One or all of the following:

- ▓ **To energize group members and have fun.**
- ▓ **To encourage the use of various strengths, e.g. verbal ability, numeric ability, visual problem solving, etc.**
- ▓ **To encourage creativity.**

TIME REQUIRED: 15 minutes

OVERVIEW

The "Team Triathlon" in the original *Games Teams Play* was so popular that other versions have been provided.

Each of the three challenges in a Team Triathlon requires a different skill set or aptitude. This variety stretches participants' minds in several directions and ensures that most, if not all participants will be able to contribute strongly in at least one of the challenges.

The rules for each triathlon are identical. The group is organized into teams of six to 10 members (ideally). Teams receive three envelopes, each containing a different challenge.

The game is competitive and teams win based on the number of correct answers and their speed (teams receive bonus points for finishing first).

On the signal from the facilitator, teams open the envelope marked Challenge #1. Once they have solved the problem, they send a runner to the facilitator with their answer. If it is correct, they move on to the envelope marked Challenge #2. If not, they must try again. (If

several teams have moved on and one or two are stumped, you may suggest that they too move ahead. They will not receive the point for that activity.)

Once they have solved as many brain teasers as possible in the envelope marked Challenge #2, they move to Challenge #3. However, once they set an envelope aside, they can't return to it.

When they have completed Challenge #3, they signal that they are finished by singing a loud round of a simple song, e.g. *Three Blind Mice*.

SCORING

Teams receive one point for each correct answer, plus two points for finishing first— i.e. *beginning* to sing the song first.

MATERIALS REQUIRED

- Instructions (one sheet per participant).
- Three or four copies of each of the three challenges selected for each group.
- Three envelopes for each group.

PREPARATION

Copy The Team Triathlon—Instructions (Handout H20.1) and Challenges selected (H20.2, 3 and 4) and put challenges into envelopes. Number each envelope according to the number of the challenge inside, i.e. Challenge #1, etc.

STEPS

1. Distribute the instructions and envelopes.
2. Review the instructions with the group.
3. Conduct the game.

ANSWERS

Challenge #1—post.
Challenge #2

1. Twosome.
2. Repeat performance.
3. Nose dive.
4. Banana split.

Your Notes

5. Down draft.
6. Down in the dumps.
7. Cross-section.
8. Feeling under the weather.

Challenge #3— $\frac{14}{10}$

Explanation—Adding 3 to each denominator results in the following numerator. Adding 3 to each numerator results in the following denominator. Therefore $\frac{14}{10}$ follows $\frac{7}{11}$.

Your Notes

THE TEAM TRIATHLON B— INSTRUCTIONS

1. You will receive a set of three envelopes. Your task as a group is to complete each of the challenges presented in the envelopes as accurately and quickly as possible.

2. Wait until the leader signals to open Challenge #1. When you have an answer to the problem presented, assign a team member to check your answer with the leader. If you have the correct answer, go on to Challenge #2. If not try again.

3. Envelope #2 contains several brain teasers. Once you have solved as many brain teasers as possible, go on to Challenge #3. **Note: You may not return to an earlier challenge once you have set it aside.**

4. When you have solved the last challenge (Challenge #3), signal that you are finished by loudly singing a verse of _____ _____.

TEAM TRIATHLON B— CHALLENGE #1

Find what each of the following words has in common.

sign

letter

score

Common denominator: _____

Handout
H20.3

TEAM TRIATHLON B— CHALLENGE #2

Solve each of the following brain teasers by determining the phrase depicted.

1. **some**
   some

2. performance performance

3. N
   O
   S
   E
   ∨

4. **ban   ana**

5. **D**
   R
   A
   F
   T

6. **ddownumps**

7. s
   e
   c
   s e c t i o n
   i
   o
   n

8. **weather**
   feeling

TEAM TRIATHLON B— CHALLENGE #3

Insert the missing numbers:

$$\frac{1}{5} \quad \frac{8}{4} \quad \frac{7}{11} \quad \frac{?}{?}$$

Answer: _____

GAME 21 TEAM TRIATHLON C

OBJECTIVES

One or all of the following:

■ **To energize group members and have fun.**

■ **To encourage the use of various strengths, e.g. verbal ability, numeric ability, visual problem solving, etc.**

■ **To encourage creativity.**

TIME REQUIRED: 15 minutes

OVERVIEW

The "Team Triathlon" in the original *Games Teams Play* was so popular that other versions have been provided.

Each of the three challenges in a Team Triathlon requires a different skill set or aptitude. This variety stretches participants' minds in several directions and ensures that most, if not all participants will be able to contribute strongly in at least one of the challenges.

The rules for each triathlon are identical. The group is organized into teams of six to 10 members (ideally). Teams receive three envelopes, each containing a different challenge.

The game is competitive and teams win based on the number of correct answers and their speed (teams receive bonus points for finishing first).

On the signal from the facilitator, teams open the envelope marked Challenge #1. Once they have solved the problem, they send a runner to the facilitator with their answer. If it is correct, they move on to the envelope marked Challenge #2. If not, they must try again. (If several teams have moved on and one or two are stumped, you may suggest that they too move ahead. They will not receive the point for that activity.)

Your Notes

From *More Games Teams Play* by Leslie Bendaly © 2000, McGraw-Hill Ryerson.

Once they have solved as many brain teasers as possible in the envelope marked Challenge #2, they move to Challenge #3. However, once they set an envelope aside, they can't return to it.

When they have completed Challenge #3, they signal that they are finished by singing a loud round of a simple song, e.g. *Three Blind Mice*.

SCORING

Teams receive one point for each correct answer, plus two points for finishing first— i.e. *beginning* to sing the song first.

MATERIALS REQUIRED

- Instructions (one sheet per participant).
- Three or four copies of each of the three challenges selected for each group.
- Three envelopes for each group.

PREPARATION

Copy The Team Triathlon—Instructions (Handout H21.1) and Challenges selected (H21.2, 3 and 4) and put challenges into envelopes. Number each envelope according to the number of the challenge inside, i.e. Challenge #1, etc.

STEPS

1. Distribute the instructions and envelopes.
2. Review the instructions with the group.
3. Conduct the game.

ANSWERS

Challenge #1—frame.

Challenge #2

1. Double duty.
2. Heavy rain.
3. Ear infection.
4. Overheated engine.
5. High hopes.
6. Without a second thought.
7. A house divided.
8. Reversed roles.

Challenge #3—4.

Explanation—Each column adds up to 9.

Your Notes

THE TEAM TRIATHLON C— INSTRUCTIONS

1. You will receive a set of three envelopes. Your task as a group is to complete each of the challenges presented in the envelopes as accurately and quickly as possible.

2. Wait until the leader signals to open Challenge #1. When you have an answer to the problem presented, assign a team member to check your answer with the leader. If you have the correct answer, go on to Challenge #2. If not try again.

3. Envelope #2 contains several brain teasers. Once you have solved as many brain teasers as possible, go on to Challenge #3. **Note: You may not return to an earlier challenge once you have set it aside.**

4. When you have solved the last challenge (Challenge #3), signal that you are finished by loudly singing a verse of _____ _____.

TEAM TRIATHLON C— CHALLENGE #1

Find what each of the following words has in common.

picture

door

car

Common denominator: _____

Handout
H21.3

TEAM TRIATHLON C— CHALLENGE #2

Solve each of the following brain teasers by determining the phrase depicted.

1. duty duty

2. RAIN

3. fectearion

4. engine
heated

5. HOPES

6. 1 thought
2
3 thought
4 thought

7. ho use

8. selor

Handout
H21.4

TEAM TRIATHLON C— CHALLENGE #3

Insert the missing number:

4	1	2
2	6	3
3	2	?

GAME 22 TEAM TRIATHLON D

OBJECTIVES

One or all of the following:

- **To energize group members and have fun.**
- **To encourage the use of various strengths, e.g. verbal ability, numeric ability, visual problem solving, etc.**
- **To encourage creativity.**

TIME REQUIRED: 15 minutes

OVERVIEW

The "Team Triathlon" in the original *Games Teams Play* was so popular that other versions have been provided.

Each of the three challenges in a Team Triathlon requires a different skill set or aptitude. This variety stretches participants' minds in several directions and ensures that most, if not all participants will be able to contribute strongly in at least one of the challenges.

The rules for each triathlon are identical. The group is organized into teams of six to 10 members (ideally). Teams receive three envelopes, each containing a different challenge.

The game is competitive and teams win based on the number of correct answers and their speed (teams receive bonus points for finishing first).

On the signal from the facilitator, teams open the envelope marked Challenge #1. Once they have solved the problem, they send a runner to the facilitator with their answer. If it is correct, they move on to the envelope marked Challenge #2. If not, they must try again. (If

Your Notes

several teams have moved on and one or two are stumped, you may suggest that they too move ahead. They will not receive the point for that activity.)

Once they have solved as many brain teasers as possible in the envelope marked Challenge #2, they move to Challenge #3. However, once they set an envelope aside, they can't return to it.

When they have completed Challenge #3, they signal that they are finished by singing a loud round of a simple song, e.g. *Three Blind Mice.*

SCORING

Teams receive one point for each correct answer, plus two points for finishing first— i.e. *beginning* to sing the song first.

MATERIALS REQUIRED

- Instructions (one sheet per participant).
- Three or four copies of each of the three challenges selected for each group.
- Three envelopes for each group.

PREPARATION

Copy The Team Triathlon—Instructions (Handout H22.1) and Challenges selected (H22.2, 3 and 4) and put challenges into envelopes. Number each envelope according to the number of the challenge inside, i.e. Challenge #1, etc.

STEPS

1. Distribute the instructions and envelopes.
2. Review the instructions with the group.
3. Conduct the game.

ANSWERS

Challenge #1—Silent.
Challenge #2

1. Light at the end of the tunnel.
2. Arrive on time.
3. Line up.
4. It's after the fact.
5. Copy cat.

Your Notes

6. A turn of events.

7. Love at first sight.

8. Broken rung.

Challenge #3—RD.

Explanation—The word reads 'porridge' spelled counterclockwise.

Your Notes

THE TEAM TRIATHLON D— INSTRUCTIONS

1. You will receive a set of three envelopes. Your task as a group is to complete each of the challenges presented in the envelopes as accurately and quickly as possible.

2. Wait until the leader signals to open Challenge #1. When you have an answer to the problem presented, assign a team member to check your answer with the leader. If you have the correct answer, go on to Challenge #2. If not try again.

3. Envelope #2 contains several brain teasers. Once you have solved as many brain teasers as possible, go on to Challenge #3. **Note: You may not return to an earlier challenge once you have set it aside.**

4. When you have solved the last challenge (Challenge #3), signal that you are finished by loudly singing a verse of _____ _____.

TEAM TRIATHLON D— CHALLENGE #1

Find what each of the following words has in common.

movies

partner

night

Common denominator: _____

TEAM TRIATHLON D— CHALLENGE #2

Solve each of the following brain teasers by determining the phrase depicted.

1. tunnel light

2. arrive
   —————
   time

3. e
   n
   i
   L

4. Fact it's

5. cat cat

6. EVENTS

7. Love   sight
           sight
           sight

8. run g

Handout
H22.4

TEAM TRIATHLON D— CHALLENGE #3

Insert the missing letters.

GAME 23 TEAM TRIATHLON E

OBJECTIVES

One or all of the following:

- ▓ **To energize group members and have fun.**
- ▓ **To encourage the use of various strengths, e.g. verbal ability, numeric ability, visual problem solving, etc.**
- ▓ **To encourage creativity.**

TIME REQUIRED: 15 minutes

OVERVIEW

The "Team Triathlon" in the original *Games Teams Play* was so popular that other versions have been provided.

Each of the three challenges in a Team Triathlon requires a different skill set or aptitude. This variety stretches participants' minds in several directions and ensures that most, if not all participants will be able to contribute strongly in at least one of the challenges.

The rules for each triathlon are identical. The group is organized into teams of six to 10 members (ideally). Teams receive three envelopes, each containing a different challenge.

The game is competitive and teams win based on the number of correct answers and their speed (teams receive bonus points for finishing first).

On the signal from the facilitator, teams open the envelope marked Challenge #1. Once they have solved the problem, they send a runner to the facilitator with their answer. If it is correct, they move on to the envelope marked Challenge #2. If not, they must try again. (If

> **Your Notes**

several teams have moved on and one or two are stumped, you may suggest that they too move ahead. They will not receive the point for that activity.)

Once they have solved as many brain teasers as possible in the envelope marked Challenge #2, they move to Challenge #3. However, once they set an envelope aside, they can't return to it.

When they have completed Challenge #3, they signal that they are finished by singing a loud round of a simple song, e.g. *Three Blind Mice*.

SCORING

Teams receive one point for each correct answer, plus two points for finishing first— i.e. *beginning* to sing the song first.

MATERIALS REQUIRED

- Instructions (one sheet per participant).
- Three or four copies of each of the three challenges selected for each group.
- Three envelopes for each group.

PREPARATION

Copy The Team Triathlon—Instructions (Handout H23.1) and Challenges selected (H23.2, 3 and 4) and put challenges into envelopes. Number each envelope according to the number of the challenge inside, i.e. Challenge #1, etc.

STEPS

1. Distribute the instructions and envelopes.
2. Review the instructions with the group.
3. Conduct the game.

ANSWERS

Challenge #1—Open.
Challenge #2

1. Last resort.
2. Pinup poster.
3. Countdown.

Your Notes

From *More Games Teams Play* by Leslie Bendaly © 2000, McGraw-Hill Ryerson.

4. At the end of it all.

5. Parasite.

6. All above board.

7. Slanted view.

8. Jewel in the crown.

Challenge #3—30.

Explanation—Add 3 to 6 and then add an additional 2 each time—$6 + 3 = 9$; $9 + 5 = 14$; $14 + 7 = 21$; $21 + 9 = 30$.

Your Notes

THE TEAM TRIATHLON E— INSTRUCTIONS

1. You will receive a set of three envelopes. Your task as a group is to complete each of the challenges presented in the envelopes as accurately and quickly as possible.

2. Wait until the leader signals to open Challenge #1. When you have an answer to the problem presented, assign a team member to check your answer with the leader. If you have the correct answer, go on to Challenge #2. If not try again.

3. Envelope #2 contains several brain teasers. Once you have solved as many brain teasers as possible, go on to **Challenge #3. Note: You may not return to an earlier challenge once you have set it aside.**

4. When you have solved the last challenge (Challenge #3), signal that you are finished by loudly singing a verse of _____ _____.

TEAM TRIATHLON E— CHALLENGE #1

Find what each of the following words has in common.

envelope

parachute

bottle

Common denominator: _____

TEAM TRIATHLON E— CHALLENGE #2

Solve each of the following brain teasers by determining the phrase depicted.

1. resort
   resort
   resort
   (resort)

2. N
   I
   P   POSTER

3. C
   O
   U
   N
   T

4. it all

5. site site

6.   all
   board

7. *View*

8. crjewelown

Handout
H23.4

TEAM TRIATHLON E— CHALLENGE #3

Insert the missing number.

GAME 24 WHAT ARE YOU MISSING?

OBJECTIVE

■ To emphasize the importance of connecting with the larger team.

TIME REQUIRED: 10 minutes

BACKGROUND

Most team members intellectually understand the need to connect with people outside of their immediate team—members of the larger team, but many do not do it. They may be too busy or simply do not think of people with whom they do not work closely.

In this workout, teams are asked to each put together a puzzle. It may be in either of the following forms:

- A purchased jigsaw puzzle of about 30 pieces.
- A jigsaw puzzle that you create by putting a statement describing a current team or organizational problem on a piece of cardboard in large letters and then cutting it into pieces.

MATERIALS REQUIRED

- One puzzle of either of the above choices for each group.

PREPARATION

Remove a puzzle piece from each set of puzzle pieces and replace each with two different pieces from another puzzle. Each puzzle should be missing one piece and have two pieces of another.

STEPS

1. If working with one large team, divide members into smaller groups of six to eight.

> **Your Notes**

2. Distribute the sets of puzzle pieces, one per group.

3. Ask each workshop group to put their puzzle together. Each group will eventually realize that they must get the missing piece from another group—they must first find the right group and then trade pieces.

4. Invite the groups to describe the game's message or theme. They may say something like, "It is important to remember to connect with people who are outside of your immediate group," *or* "People outside of your immediate team may hold knowledge or information that is vital to you."

5. Put up Overhead T24.1 with the question "What are you missing by not connecting?"

6. Invite the group to discuss the question "Why is connecting more important today than ever before?"

   Likely responses:

   - "We can no longer know everything—we have to depend on others."
   - "We must act more quickly and because of this, we must get information quickly. Connecting with others who have that information or experience is much quicker than trying to do it yourself."
   - "Our own knowledge and experience are quickly dated."

7. Tell the group that you would like them to consider the question "What are you missing by not connecting?" from both an individual perspective and a team perspective.

8. Distribute Handouts H24.1, H24.2, and H24.3.

9. Review the instructions.

10. Allow five to 10 minutes for the group to complete the Individual Workout (Handout H24.1) and 20 minutes for the Group Workout (Handout H24.2).

11. Invite teams to share their commitments to action, and ask each team member to record them on Handout H24.3.

Your Notes

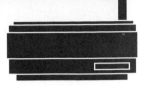

YOUR CONNECTIONS

What are you missing by not connecting?

WHAT ARE YOU MISSING?

INDIVIDUAL WORKOUT

TIME REQUIRED: 10 minutes

Identify:

1. People you don't connect with as often as you should. These are likely individuals you do not have to connect with to get your job done. They potentially add value or could make your job easier and/or you have something to offer them.

2. People you connect with but not always effectively. Perhaps you misunderstand one another or experience conflict.

List them below:

People I don't connect with as often as I should:

_____

_____

_____

_____

_____

_____

People I connect with but not always effectively:

_____

_____

_____

_____

_____

_____

WHAT ARE YOU MISSING?

GROUP WORKOUT

TIME REQUIRED: 25 minutes

1. Consider teams or individuals with whom your team would benefit from connecting: (a) more often **or** (b) more effectively. Brainstorm to develop a list for each category.

OUR TEAM WOULD BENEFIT BY CONNECTING

More often with:	**More effectively with:**
_____	_____
_____	_____
_____	_____

2. Consider what actions your team can take to better connect with the individual(s) listed.

3. Develop team commitments to action.

Handout
H24.3

COMMITMENT TO MAKING CONNECTIONS

Team Commitments to Action

GAME 25 TEAM MAKEOVER

OBJECTIVES

Any or all of the following:

- ■ **To reflect on how the team is perceived.**
- ■ **To identify how the team wants to be seen.**
- ■ **To improve the team's image.**

TIME REQUIRED: One hour

OVERVIEW

How others perceive the team in the organization can strongly affect its success. This activity asks team members to describe on paper that will be posted on a board how they believe the team is presently perceived, as well as and how they would like the team to be seen. The team then makes commitments to making over the team image.

When the activity is completed the board or wall will look like this.

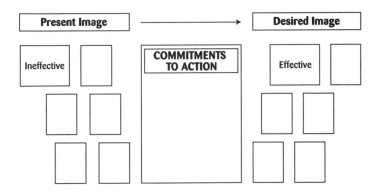

MATERIALS REQUIRED

- Colored sheets of paper large enough to write a word or phrase and be visible across the room.
- Markers or felt pens (one per participant).
- An arrow cut from colored paper.

From *More Games Teams Play* by Leslie Bendaly © 2000, McGraw-Hill Ryerson.

- The titles: "Present Image" and "Desired Image" on colored paper.
- Flipchart.

STEPS

1. Introduce the activity.

2. Distribute the colored pieces of paper and markers.

3. Ask each member to print a word or phrase that he or she thinks others in the organization would use to describe their team. Ask that they print so that the words can be read across the room

4. Ask participants to post their descriptions on one end of a wall or board under the heading "Present Image."

5. Discuss and come to consensus on the key descriptors. Remove points that are repetitive or that the team does not agree on. Recognize the positive statements and discuss any negative descriptors. You might ask: "What does the team do or not do that causes people to see the team this way?"

6. Invite participants to write a word or phrase on a colored piece of paper that they would like people to be using to describe their team.

7. Place the arrow to the right of the heading "Present Image." Ask participant to post their desired descriptions under the heading "Desired Image," as shown in the Overview. (*Note:* some descriptions will be on both sides.)

8. Have the group discuss and come to consensus on the key descriptions.

9. Ask the team to brainstorm to identify actions that the team can take to realize the desired image.

10. List the actions on a flipchart and post below the arrow under the heading "Commitments to Action."

11. Check for agreement that team members will follow through on the commitments.

Your Notes

From *More Games Teams Play* by Leslie Bendaly © 2000, McGraw-Hill Ryerson.

GAME 26 A LETTER TO YOUR TEAM

OBJECTIVES

To better understand:

■ **Team members' perceptions of the team's strengths and opportunities for improvement.**

■ **Team members' needs.**

■ **How team members see their own contribution.**

TIME REQUIRED: One hour.

BACKGROUND

This activity can provide the basis for an entire team building day or stand on its own as a shorter activity. You may use the letter in Handout H26.1 for either:

A short (perhaps one hour) team activity in which members gain a better understanding of their fellow members' needs, as well as a greater understanding of their view of the team—its strengths and opportunities for improvement.

OR

Part of a team building day to gather team members' perceptions of team strengths, opportunities for improvement, team issues and their perceived contributions. You may then use that information to design a team building workshop.

MATERIALS REQUIRED

- Copies of Handout H26.l (one per participant).
- One letter sized envelope for each member.

Your Notes

STEPS

1. Introduce the activity. You might say something like, "Letter writing has always been an effective way to share personal thoughts. When writing a letter, the author has an opportunity to reflect and take his or her time in putting together thoughts. Writing allows people to express themselves with less risk than speaking and often it allows them to be more open.

   "In order for teams to develop, openness about both our strengths and opportunities for growth is essential. I'm going to invite each of you to write a letter to your team."

   Explain that when they have written their letters, you will collect them and read them aloud.

   Note: Decide beforehand whether the authors' names should be shared at the time of reading the letters. If there is any concern about the team's climate, level of trust or the members' comfort with identifying themselves, choose the anonymous route.

2. Distribute the blank letters (Handout H26.1).

3. Give participants 10 to 15 minutes to write their letters. Emphasize that you want them to take their time and write letters that have been given careful thought.

4. Ask the group members to fold their letters. You might have them put the letters in envelopes.

5. Read each letter out loud and capture the key points under the following headings on a flipchart, board, etc.:
   - Team Strengths.
   - Opportunities for Improvement.
   - Team Members Contributions.

6. Acknowledge the team strengths.

7. Discuss the opportunities for improvement.

8. Lead the team in developing commitments to action to match the opportunities for improvement.

Your Notes

A LETTER TO YOUR TEAM

Dear Team:

Just a note to share with you some thoughts about our teamwork.

I feel good to be a member of this team because . . .

I believe I make some important contributions to the team. I . . .

I would have an even more positive team experience if . . .

If these things happened, I believe the benefits to the team would be . . .

Let's continue to work together to be the best we can be.

_____

(Your Name)

From *More Games Teams Play* by Leslie Bendaly © 2000, McGraw-Hill Ryerson.

GAME 27 THE PAUSE THAT REFRESHES

OBJECTIVE

■ To learn reflective practices to enhance the quality of team decisions.

TIME REQUIRED: One hour +

BACKGROUND

This workout can be linked to the workout My Intuition Tells Me (see page 283).

In this workout, the team will address an actual team problem or challenge. Send out notice beforehand to all team members that the purpose of this meeting or workshop is to enhance the team's problem solving ability. In the process, they will address a real team issue (state the issue or problem) and a secondary benefit of the workshop will be finding a solution to the problem or at least taking the first steps toward a solution.

Ensure that you select a problem that has already been clearly defined by the team and/or team leader. You want the group to be able to go immediately to brainstorming for solutions. Ask members in your introductory letter to reflect on the problem before the meeting, and to come to the meeting with ideas or recommendations.

In the workshop you will introduce the team to Steps for Reflective Decision-Making (Handout H27.1).

STEPS FOR REFLECTIVE DECISION-MAKING

1. Individually consider the problem (before the meeting and/or quietly at the beginning of the meeting) and its possible solutions.

Your Notes

2. Gather the ideas generated about the problem (ideas are shared without discussion).

3. Have the group discuss the ideas.

4. Take a 10 minute reflection break. Ask members not to talk. During the break members should consider:

- How am I feeling about the discussion so far?
- If there is some discomfort, why? Will whatever I am uncomfortable about affect the quality of the decision?
- Have we missed anything?
- Is an "obvious" solution emerging and how do I feel about it?

5. Return to discussion mode. "Does anyone wish to add anything?"

6. Make the decision. (You may choose to use a formal decision-making method such as weighing options against a list of criteria.)

7. Take a three minute reflection break. Note that this is not meant to encourage constant reworking of decisions, but it is an opportunity to do a quality check. It is better to do so now rather than once the team has begun to implement the decision. The group should consider the following questions:

- How am I feeling?
- If there is discomfort, why?
- Has it anything to do with the quality of the decision?
- Did we miss anything important in the process?

8. Return to the group to confirm the decision or for further discussion if something has been missed. Allow a limited time to add the new thoughts and make a final decision.

STEPS

1. Introduce the topic of the role of reflection (and intuition if you choose to address it (see Background in Game 28)) in quality decision-making.

Your Notes

Points to Emphasize:

Most decisions are made too quickly. In an environment of fast-paced change and increased competition, wise decisions are critical. But applying quick logic to yesterday's information can't produce quality decisions for an unknown tomorrow. Wisdom requires time to reflect.

Reflection doesn't have to take a great deal of time. It requires participants get out of the convergent decision-making mode for a few minutes and let their mind wander over the issue and options.

2. Introduce the steps as described in Handout H27.1 and show the Overhead T27.1.

3. Lead the team through the steps described in Handout H27.1 using the pre-selected team problem.

4. Examine the process. You might use the following questions as discussion triggers:

   - How did reflecting affect your decision-making process?
   - How was it different from your usual decision-making processes?
   - Would the solution have been different without the reflection?

Occasionally the answer to one or more of the above questions is no. First check whether everyone in the group agrees with the "no." If so, ask if there were any other benefits from the reflection time.

Likely responses:

   - "There is a greater sense of confidence that we've made the right decision."
   - "Because people have had time to think it through, there is a greater sense of buy-in."
   - "We've identified and considered in advance all the possible obstacles."

5. Review the steps and reinforce them for future use.

Your Notes

STEPS FOR REFLECTIVE DECISION-MAKING —WORKOUT

1. Individually consider the problem (before the meeting and/or quietly at the beginning of the meeting) and its possible solutions.

2. Gather the ideas generated about the problem (without discussion).

3. Discuss the ideas.

4. Take a 10 minute reflection break. There should be no talking. During the break, members should consider:

   - How am I feeling about the discussion so far?

   - If there is some discomfort, why? Will whatever I am uncomfortable about affect the quality of the decision?

   - Have we missed anything?

   - Is an "obvious" solution emerging and how do I feel about it?

5. Return to discussion mode. Do you wish to add anything?

(continued)

6. Make the decision. (You may want to use a formal decision-making method such as weighing the options against a list of criteria.)

7. Take a three minute reflection break. Remember this is not done to encourage constantly reworking decisions, but as an opportunity to do a quality check. Consider the following questions:

   • How am I feeling?

   • If there is discomfort, why?

   • Has it anything to do with the quality of the decision?

   • Did we miss anything important in the process?

8. Return to the group to confirm the decision or for further discussion if something has been missed. Allow a limited time to add new thoughts and make a final decision.

STEPS FOR REFLECTIVE DECISION-MAKING

1. Individually consider the problem.

2. Gather everyone's ideas (without discussion).

3. Discuss the ideas.

4. Take a 10 minute reflection break.

5. Return to the discussion mode.

6. Make the decision.

7. Take a three minute reflection break.

8. Regroup to confirm the decision or continue the discussion, allowing a limited time to make a decision.

GAME 28 MY INTUITION TELLS ME*

OBJECTIVES

One or all of the following:

- ▓ **To enhance team members' awareness of intuition.**
- ▓ **To learn steps to better tap team intuition in problem solving.**

TIME REQUIRED: 45 minutes +

MATERIALS REQUIRED

- • Overhead T28.1.

BACKGROUND

Organizations, teams and individuals used to get by using logic alone to solve their problems. When the pace of change was slower and competition less fierce, logic was good enough. But applying logic which comes from yesterday's experience to information that was collected yesterday is not good enough to create superior decisions for an unknown tomorrow. Teams today must make *wise* decisions. Wisdom is created by mixing logic, information and intuition.

Throughout history, people who have achieved greatness have recognized the importance of intuition.

> **"I never discovered anything with my rational mind."**
>
> **Einstein**

Modern decision-makers are acknowledging that they can never gather all of the

---

This activity was inspired by Laura Day's book, Practical Intuition.

From *More Games Teams Play* by Leslie Bendaly © 2000, McGraw-Hill Ryerson.

Your Notes

information and still make a timely decision. They must use their intuition.

> "The dilemma of any statesman is that he can never be certain about the probable course of events. In reaching a decision, he must inevitably act on the basis of an intuition that is inherently unprovable. If he insists on certainty, he runs the danger of becoming a prisoner of events."
>
> Henry Kissinger
> Quoted by Nikola Phillips,
> **From Vision to Beyond Teamwork**

People complain that it takes too long to make decisions. In my experience, the opposite is true. A flawed process may lead to wheel spinning but otherwise decisions are often made too quickly. Because of time and other pressures, a decision is pounced on. Reflection time that allows ideas to steep and allows intuitive ideas to be recognized, greatly enhances team decision-making.

Intuition sometimes appears unbeckoned. However, heavy workloads, speed and an overload of information stifle intuition. Individuals and teams are beginning to recognize that intuition can be called upon to assist in decision-making.

Here are the steps for tapping your intuition:

1. Relax.

2. Ask a specific question.

3. Let your mind wander away from the question and the issue at hand (approximately three minutes).

4. Jot down the thoughts and pictures that went through your mind.

5. Return to the issue and weigh the possibilities with the thoughts from Step 4 in mind.

This workout provides what most groups find is a "fun" activity to which to apply these steps. They are asked to predict with the assistance of intuition the winner of a horse race with *no* prior knowledge.

Your Notes

From *More Games Teams Play* by Leslie Bendaly © 2000, McGraw-Hill Ryerson.

Assess your group before using this activity. Highly task-oriented individuals may be skeptical. Think about how you can introduce it so as to increase their receptivity. (You may decide that a group is so pragmatic that the chances of success are hampered. This, of course, is a group that would likely most benefit from better tapping their individual intuition. Weigh the risks against the benefits.)

The following suggestions will help you increase the group's receptivity.

1. Use a strong introduction to the concept of intuition which includes examples of pragmatic leaders such as Kissinger who acknowledge its importance.

2. Introduce the exercise "lightly." Acknowledge that some individuals may find the activity a little "far out" (or whatever similar description that your particular group uses). Ask them to bear with you and give it a try.

3. Emphasize that this workout is not meant to test intuition but to try out a method for better tapping it. This exercise assists in developing intuition and results are not always seen immediately. (It is likely, however, that you will have participants whose intuition is remarkably on the mark in this workout.)

TIP

Try this workout with colleagues or family members before using it in a workshop.

STEPS

1. Introduce the concept of intuition and its importance in decision making. Use information which is provided in the Background. In your discussion, you might also share examples of personal intuition and/or invite group members to share examples of how they use their intuition.

2. Introduce the five Steps for Tapping Intuition in Decision-Making (Overhead T28.1):

Your Notes

1. Relax.
2. Ask a specific question.
3. Let your mind wander away from the question or the issue at hand (approximately three minutes).
4. Jot down the thoughts and pictures that went through your mind.
5. Return to the issue and weigh the possibilities with the thoughts from the previous step in mind.

3. Lead the group through the five steps using the following:

   (a) Introduce the question "Which is the winning horse that (facilitator's name) has in mind?" Emphasize the need to be specific in the wording of the question.

   (b) Emphasize that participants are to let their minds wander away from the topic of horses and horse races. Ask that there be no talking. If lights are glaring, you may dim them. Allow approximately three minutes of quiet.

   (c) Ask participants to jot down the thoughts and pictures that went through their minds.

   (d) Present the list of horses (Overhead T28.2).

   (e) Ask participants to examine the list of horses considering their thoughts and mind pictures from the previous steps. (Note that at this point, logic is being used.)

4. Ask the group, "Does anyone see any link between any of your thoughts and ideas and the names on this list?"

5. Announce the order in which the horses placed in the race:

   1. Indian Soul
   2. Kerfoot Silver
   3. Ray Poosay
   4. Rabbit in a Hat
   5. Frosty Meadow
   6. Britannia Standard

Your Notes

Emphasize that if participants connected their thoughts with any of the horses, let alone the winners, they were listening well to their intuition.

6. Ask the participants to reflect once again, now that they have the names of the winners, on the thoughts that went through their minds. Ask the group to form small groups and to share their observations with one another. (Some people are hesitant to acknowledge their intuition successes and tend to more readily do so in a smaller group.)

7. Invite small groups to share any observations.

8. Re-emphasize that the steps they experienced are intended to develop their ability to tune into their intuition. Wind-up by briefly reviewing the five Steps.

Your Notes

STEPS FOR TAPPING INTUITION IN DECISION-MAKING

1. Relax.

2. Ask a specific question.

3. Let your mind wander away from the question or issue at hand.

4. Jot down the thoughts and pictures that went through your mind.

5. Return to the issue and weigh the possibilities with the thoughts from the previous step in mind.

THE HORSES

Britannia Standard

Kerfoot Silver

Frosty Meadow

Ray Poosay

Indian Soul

Rabbit in a Hat

GAME 29 | THE BEAUTY 4U DILEMMA

OBJECTIVES

One or all of the following:

- ▓ **To team build.**
- ▓ **To experience the challenge of decision-making when team members have differing priorities and differing personal values.**

TIME REQUIRED: Two hours

MATERIALS REQUIRED

- Handouts H29.1 and H29.2.

OVERVIEW

Participants are asked to assume the role of employees of the Beauty 4U company. An error has been made in the manufacturing of one of the company's products which leads to financial and ethical dilemmas. Participants must examine the problem and attempt to come to consensus on a solution. See Handout H29.1 for more details. This activity encourages the surfacing of different priorities and personal values.

The group is divided into four sub-groups or divisions—marketing, finance, public relations and production. Each group is asked to hold an emergency meeting and to come to consensus on a recommendation to be made to the whole management group of which they are members. Their choices are:

- Pull the product from shelves and replace the stock with new product and announce that any product purchased previous to the replacement should be returned.
- Pull the stock from the shelves and replace it with new stock.

Your Notes

- Leave the product on the shelves but replace the stock in the warehouse.
- Do nothing—carry on and make changes in the next product run (once the remaining stock is sold).
- Pull the product and discontinue it.
- Other.

Once the divisional teams have met, they take their recommendation to the larger management team (of which they are members) and work together to come to agreement on a Beauty 4U strategy to solve their problem.

STEPS

1. Describe the Beauty 4U dilemma using information from the Overview.

2. Distribute The Beauty 4U Scenario, Handout H29.1 and The Beauty 4U Dilemma—Instructions, Handout H29.2.

3. Assign group members to four Beauty 4U divisional teams:

   (a) Marketing.

   (b) Finance.

   (c) Production.

   (d) Public Relations and Communication.

4. Review instructions and allow 40 minutes for the divisional meetings.

> **TIP**
>
> Write the four division names on tent cards on meeting tables to remind participants of the role of their team.

5. Debrief the activity with the individual groups. Consider the following questions:

   - Was reaching a consensus easy or difficult? If it was easy, what contributed to a positive consensus process? If it was not easy, what hindered the consensus process?
   - Did the issues discussed focus on different personal values and common purposes, e.g. marketing, production, etc.?

6. Bring the teams together into a larger Beauty 4U management meeting.

Your Notes

From *More Games Teams Play* by Leslie Bendaly © 2000, McGraw-Hill Ryerson.

7. Assign someone to play the role of the President.

8. Ask the group to come to a Beauty 4U management decision as to how to deal with their problem. *Note:* This is designed for a group of approximately 20 people. If the group is larger, organize the group into several companies, each with four divisions.

9. Debrief once again:

    (a) Again explore the difficulty or ease with which the group came to consensus. Discussion is likely to include:

    - Bringing personal values and divisional priorities to the table.
    - The need to focus on the larger company picture.
    - The need to agree on company priorities and values.
    - The need to develop company focused decision-making criteria based on those priorities.

    (b) Identify as a group how this experience relates to the real workplace.

    (c) Recap key learning. Note that decision-making was easy as long as everyone applied the stated corporate values. If people based decisions on other values and/or divisional priorities, consensus was very difficult.

Your Notes

THE BEAUTY 4U SCENARIO

Your company, Beauty 4U, researches, develops, manufactures and sells natural beauty products. A young company, you have grown quickly, as the trend toward natural products has grown in recent years.

Cash flow is tight. Start-up costs are still being carried, as the company decided to go "first class all the way." In addition to reaching clients via the traditional route through health food stores and pharmacies, Beauty 4U also embraced e-commerce and sells products directly to the consumer through a web site. However, the company has surpassed targets for the past three years, and you are in the process of going public, anticipating the company's launch onto the stock exchange. Beauty 4U has developed a high profile and positive image as a result of creative and aggressive marketing, as well as by providing the highest quality products which have gained a loyal following of both retailers and consumers.

The tag line on your logo is "Natural products you can trust."

Your company has recently launched, with much fanfare and a very large marketing budget, a new face cream which in clinical studies demonstrated an amazing ability to decrease lines and firm skin in a few short weeks. Since strong sales were projected and the product has a long shelf life, thousands of bottles of the product have been produced. It has quickly become a best selling product.

(continued)

However, during a quality check it was discovered that an error was made in manufacturing. The ingredient that is responsible for the most dramatic skin affects, Ingredient X, was inadvertently replaced with another ingredient, Y. Ingredient Y will not only render the cream useless, but it also has a drying component that could age the skin.

BEAUTY 4U MISSION STATEMENT

Beauty 4U is committed to being the world's leading provider of the highest quality natural beauty products. Our success will be evident in satisfied customers, employees and shareholders.

THE BEAUTY 4U DILEMMA— INSTRUCTIONS

1. You will be assigned to a small divisional management team: one of either marketing; finance; public relations and communication; or production.

2. In your divisional team, come to consensus on the best next step for Beauty 4U. Here are some of your options:

   - Pull the product from shelves and replace the stock with new product and announce that any product purchased previous to the replacement should be returned.

   - Pull the stock from the shelves and replace it with new stock.

   - Leave the product on the shelves but replace the stock in the warehouse.

   - Do nothing—carry on and make changes in the next product run (once the remaining stock is sold).

   - Pull the product and discontinue it.

   - Other.

3. Be prepared to take your decision in the form of a recommendation to the larger management team.

GAME 30

WIN AS MUCH AS YOU CAN

Handle With Care ⚡

OBJECTIVES

One or all of the following:

■ **To explore issues of trust.**

■ **To learn how to prevent conflict.**

■ **To emphasize the importance of keeping the "big" team (larger organizational team) in mind.**

TIME REQUIRED: 1.5 to two hours

MATERIALS REQUIRED

- Handouts H30.1 and H30.2 (H30.3 is optional)
- Poker chips and dollars
- Envelope or pouch

OVERVIEW

This workshop provides a powerful learning experience. As in most powerful experiences, however, there are risks attached. This game creates a situation that holds potential for conflict. It requires a seasoned facilitator to lead the workshop and sufficient time for thorough discussion and resolution of any issues that might emerge.

The objective, as the title suggests, is to "win as much as you can." Participants are broken into four groups. The game consists of four rounds. In each round, each group must make a decision to choose a blue chip or a red chip. Group members make their decision based on the possible outcomes described in Handout H30.2 (read H30.2 carefully before proceeding). They will consider the information presented in H30.2 combined with their expectation of what other teams will select. For example, will all teams realize that if each team selects

Your Notes

a blue chip, everyone will win and therefore the collective whole (all teams) will gain more altogether? Or will each team play for itself and go for the biggest individual win? *Note:* Do not share this information with teams beforehand.

Each group is given eight pieces to play with —four red and four blue (the pieces may be small squares cut from cardboard, poker chips or bingo markers). Each team also receives $7. This can be in the form of seven $1 bills or coins in play or real money, seven chocolate coins or seven poker chips (if poker chips are used, choose a color other than red or blue).

For each round, each of the four groups is asked to choose a red or blue chip. Their choices are shared only with the facilitator. Groups do not know what others have chosen until the end of the round.

The facilitator shares limited information and allows no discussion at the beginning.

Information to be Shared by the Facilitator

Start the game by announcing the following:

"Your objective is to win as much as you can. You try to win by choosing a red or blue chip. You will base your decision on the Win As Much As You Can Pay Out Sheet (Handout H30.2) in front of you and what you know or assume about the other groups. You will gain more knowledge about the others as the game progresses.

"You will have four rounds in which to 'Win As Much As You Can.' During each round, you will discuss your options with your team members and come to agreement on your selection. At the end of each round I will come to your group to collect the blue or red chip you have selected. You will slip your choice into this envelope (or pouch) and no one will know another team's decision until the end of the round. After the first round, we will share a little information with one another as to why each group made the selection they did. After the second round, you will appoint one of your group members to represent your group in negotiating a deal for you. The representative will be given five minutes to strike a deal with the other three negotiators that will allow you to 'Win As Much As You Can' in round three.

"When your representative returns to your group, he or she must then get you to support the agreement made.

"We will then play round three. After round three, you have another opportunity to negotiate a deal that allows you to 'Win As Much As You Can' in round four. You may have the same negotiator represent you or appoint a new one."

What to Expect

If each individual group chose blue each time, each group would end up with $11 or $44 in total for the entire group (each group started with $7, plus $1 for each of the four rounds). It is evident (although not always immediately) that the only way for *everyone* to win is for *everyone* to select a blue chip.

However, participants usually see blue as a risk because they don't trust that everyone will choose blue. Red is the lower risk choice and offers the potential of allowing an individual group to win more than the other groups.

Participants often interpret the *You* in "Win As Much As You Can" as representing their individual group, rather than the collective whole.

The prevailing interpretation of the game's objective is often not "Win As Much As You Can" but win more than the others (or beat them).

Groups who select the blue chips experience frustration that:

- Others can't see "the obvious" that an unanimous blue choice means everyone wins; and
- That others don't trust enough to select blue.

Your Notes

Frustration often increases when groups renege on the agreement that their negotiator made in the agreement. (Usually the agreement is that everyone will choose blue.) When groups renege, they usually renege for one of three reasons:

1. They don't trust that other groups will keep the agreement; or

2. They may have chosen blue in the first or second round when others didn't and now have lost their faith or want to get even; or

3. The group is still interpreting the objective "Win As Much As You Can" to mean that they must "beat" the others and therefore anything goes.

The facilitator's challenges in the debrief include:

- Helping people work through any negative emotions that may have emerged;
- Protecting the group(s) that renege (they are usually embarrassed when they realize that they were interpreting the game differently and as a result may be seen critically by others);
- Helping the group understand that the real issue is not lack of trust but lack of common understanding and lack of open communication which lead to lack of trust and conflict. If these conditions had been present at the beginning, it is likely that each group would have selected the blue chip each time.

More detailed instructions and information are provided under Steps below.

Note: It is likely that someone will ask you at early stages of the game whether "Win As Much As You Can" refers to the individual groups or the whole group. Tell them they must decide that for themselves.

MATERIALS

- Dollars or poker chips representing dollars for each group (seven dollars for each of four groups equals 28 dollars in total) plus

Your Notes

10 for the facilitator's bank. They are seldom used but are needed "just in case." The total number of single dollars required is 38.

- Game pieces—four blue and four red for each group for a total of 16 blue and 16 red poker chips, bingo markers or small squares of heavy paper.
- One envelope or pouch for each team to hold the game pieces.
- One envelope or pouch for the facilitator to collect the game pieces for a total five envelopes or pouches.
- Win As Much As You Can Instructions (Handout H30.1) for each participant.
- Win As Much As You Can Pay Out Sheet (Handout H30.2).
- Take Away Key Learning Points sheet (Handout H30.3) (optional).

PREPARATION

1. Gather or purchase 32 game pieces (16 blue and 16 red) and 38 single dollars or chips.

2. Copy Handouts H30.1 and H30.2 (enough for one of each per person).

3. Purchase prizes (optional).

STEPS

1. Distribute Handouts H30.1 and H30.2.

2. Review the instructions with the group and share the information provided under Information to be Shared by the Facilitator (above).

3. Begin Round 1. Allow groups five to 10 minutes to come to agreement on their choice of red or blue game piece to submit. (You will allow less time in future rounds. In this round participants need a few minutes to understand the game.)

4. Collect the responses from each group. Have each group slip the game piece of their choice into your envelope or pouch.

5. Once you have collected all four game pieces, share the results with a bit of fan-fare. You might ask what they predict will be the outcome. Pull the four game pieces out one by one from the envelope or pouch, holding each one up for the group to see. If there is only one red or blue chip, save it until last to build up the suspense.

6. Collect and/or distribute dollars based on the pay-out formula explained in Handout H30.2.

7. Invite a small amount of discussion. Ask each group why they made the choice they did.

8. Tell the participants that they now have access to additional information. They know how one another is thinking. Remind them that the objective of the game is to "Win As Much As You Can."

9. In Round 2, allow five minutes of decision-making time.

10. Collect the game pieces and pay-out dollars as in Steps 4, 5 and 6 above.

11. Ask each group to select one of their members to act as their negotiator.

12. Allow five minutes for the groups to brief their negotiator on the deal they would like him or her to make.

13. Allow negotiators between five and seven minutes to strike a deal with one another.

14. Ask negotiators to explain the deal to their group and check for consensus/support from their group.

15. Move into Round 3 and visit each group and collect the game pieces (red or blue) they have selected (repeat Steps 4, 5 and 6).

16. It is likely that one or more groups have reneged. Whatever the outcome, invite discussion.

You might ask:
"How do you feel about the outcome?"

From *More Games Teams Play* by Leslie Bendaly © 2000, McGraw-Hill Ryerson.

If the groups happen to come to agreement at this stage, the likely response is "great."

If at least one group has reneged, responses are likely to include: "hurt," "disappointed," "angry," and "frustrated."

Lead a dialogue between those who followed through on the commitment and those who didn't. Those who reneged will likely respond:

"We didn't think we could trust you."

"We interpreted the "you" in the objective to refer to individual groups and we thought we were supposed to do whatever would allow us to win."

You might ask the groups who chose blue how they feel about the upcoming final round.

Likely response:
"We don't trust them."

This can lead to a discussion about the difficulty in rebuilding trust.

You might ask:
"How can we rebuild trust in this case?"

Responses often include:
"Play the last round and ensure that everyone lives up to the agreement."

17. Play Round 4.

18. It is highly unlikely that any group will renege. Whatever the outcome, emphasize that:

- This game is designed to encourage people to choose red and therefore to raise questions of trust and to create potential conflict. The individuals and their personal values did not create the potential conflict—it resulted from a flawed process.

- Invite people to identify ways in which the process was flawed. Participants are likely to respond:

"You didn't clarify the objective or give us an opportunity to discuss it."

Your Notes

"We didn't have a chance to develop any working agreements."

"You didn't allow us to communicate between groups in the beginning and limited the communication after that."

"We didn't have full participation. You had us select negotiators who spoke for us and who then had to get us to support an agreement we hadn't participated in."

If any of the above possibilities are missed, point them out to the group.

- Ask the group to discuss how the process led to distrust and potential conflict.

  Likely observations:

  "We didn't clarify the objective or communicate and therefore each group interpreted the game in their own way."

  "We expected others to interpret it the same way."

  "We expected others to behave the way we did."

  "Because we couldn't communicate openly, we weren't sure that we could trust them."

  "You set us up in separate teams which suggested to us that we were playing individually."

- Tally the total winnings. It is likely that they will have won less in total than they could have won if all groups had chosen blue and played as a whole from the beginning.

20. Encourage the transfer of learning among the group participants. Invite participants to apply the above discussion to the workplace.

21. Invite participants to recap their key learning. Depending on your objective in using this game, you might ask them to capture the key points on the "Key Learning Points" sheet (Handout H30.3).

Your Notes

From *More Games Teams Play* by Leslie Bendaly © 2000, McGraw-Hill Ryerson.

WIN AS MUCH AS YOU CAN— INSTRUCTIONS

Your objective is to "Win As Much As You Can."

You will be given $7 to play with. You have four rounds in which to Win As Much As You Can.

In each round, you will be asked to make a simple decision (to choose a blue or red game piece). You will make your decision based on the "Pay Out Sheet" (Handout H30.2) provided, your knowledge or perception of the other groups and what you might expect them to choose.

The facilitator will visit your team in each round and ask you to put a game piece of the color of your choice in his or her envelope or pouch. Take care that other teams cannot see your selection.

After Rounds 1 and 3, you will choose one of your members to act as a negotiator for your team. Their job will be to make a deal with the other groups that will allow you to Win As Much As You Can, in Rounds 3 and 4.

(continued)

Handout
H30.1
(cont'd)

GAME OVERVIEW

Round 1   Each group chooses a red or blue game piece which will be collected by the facilitator. Results are tallied and money collected or distributed.

Round 2   Each group chooses a red or blue game piece which will be collected by the facilitator. Results are tallied and money collected or distributed.

NEGOTIATIONS

Round 3   Each group chooses a red or blue game piece which will be collected by the facilitator. Results are tallied and money collected or distributed.

NEGOTIATIONS

Round 4   Each group chooses a red or blue game piece which will be collected by the facilitator. Results are tallied and money collected or distributed.

PAY OUT SHEET

HOW YOU WIN (OR LOSE)

Possible Combinations	Wins and Losses
	Each group that chooses:
If 4 groups choose **red** chips	**red** loses $1
If 3 groups choose **red** chips and 1 group chooses **blue** chip	**red** wins $1 **blue** loses $3
If 2 groups choose **red** chips and 2 groups choose **blue** chips	**red** wins $2 **blue** loses $2
If 1 group chooses **red** chip and 3 groups choose **blue** chips	**red** wins $3 **blue** loses $1
If 4 groups choose **blue** chips	**blue** wins $1

Handout
H30.3

KEY LEARNING POINTS

_____

_____

_____

_____

_____

_____

_____

_____

_____

_____

_____

_____

_____

_____

_____

_____

GAME 31 EARTHQUAKE
Handle With Care

OBJECTIVES

One or all of the following:

- ▪ **To learn how to work more effectively together in spite of different values or priorities.**
- ▪ **To better understand the importance of effective dialogue.**
- ▪ **To strengthen team consensus reaching skills.**

TIME REQUIRED: 1.5 hours

OVERVIEW

This activity brings personal values to the forefront. The group is asked to make decisions that for some may be sensitive.

The workshop group(s) is asked to take the role of a team of tour organizers who have taken a group to an excavation site on a Greek Island. Six adventurous members of the group have gone down a narrow passage into an ancient tomb. There has been a mild earthquake, potentially dangerous for the group trapped below. No one has been hurt but the only entrance passage (the one through which they entered the tomb) has collapsed and water is running into the tomb. There is a possibility that some may drown. A rescue team is on its way. They have given the organizers one instruction—they are to list the names of the trapped individuals in the order in which they will be pulled out so there will be no confusion and wasted time at the time of rescue. It may take some time to get each person out. There may not be sufficient time to rescue everyone. The organizers have the name of each tour group member but only sketchy information beyond that.

Your Notes

The challenge the participants will face—to be discussed after the activity, not before—is how to come to consensus when perspectives on an issue and the accompanying values are very different. Participants will find that in order to accomplish the task, they must be able to agree on a method for making the decision.

The struggle that most groups face is that some members may feel that they shouldn't be making this kind of a decision at all. They will contend that "We have no right to place more value on one life than another." They will suggest a method that doesn't consider the individual descriptions at all—such as drawing names from a hat. Other members may argue that it is "our responsibility to make the best and most rational decision possible. And so, although no one likes putting more value on one person, we must try to find criteria by which we can make our decision."

Some groups don't get past this first step and never develop a list. Those who agree that they should use criteria still have to get agreement within the group on which criteria to use.

Groups which produce lists before the rescue team arrives are those whose members adopt a random method of decision-making such as drawing names from a hat and those groups which agree quickly on criteria and are able to apply them in the allotted time of 30 minutes.

MATERIALS REQUIRED

- Handout H31.1—one for each participant.
- Handout H31.2—one for each small group.
- Handout H31.3—one for each participant.

STEPS

1. Distribute Handouts:
   - H31.1: Earthquake—The Scenario and Instructions.
   - H31.2: Observer's Guide.
   - H31.3: Reflections.

Your Notes

From *More Games Teams Play* by Leslie Bendaly © 2000, McGraw-Hill Ryerson.

2. Review the handouts and ask someone in each group to volunteer to be the Process Observer. The Observer will focus his or her attention on the group process with particular attention given to the points outlined in the Observer's Guide Handout (H31.2). The Observer will share observations with his or her group at the end of the activity.

3. Conduct the activity.

4. Debrief.

(a) Ask the Observers to share observations with their groups.

(b) Ask each group whether they reached consensus. Invite those who reached consensus to share what they did that helped them reach consensus.

Include Observers' comments.

Likely responses:

- "We genuinely listened to one another."
- "Most tried not to 'shoot down' others' ideas."
- "We all agreed that they couldn't 'play God'."
- "We found a method that you were all happy with (perhaps pulling names from a hat)."
- "We all agreed on a few criteria, e.g. women and children first; those with dependents first; youngest first."

(c) Ask groups that did not reach consensus what hindered them. Include Observers' comments.

Likely responses:

- "We could not agree on a decision-making method."
- "Our points of view were too different and no one was willing to move from their position."
- "We didn't try to understand others' points of view—we were just trying to sell our own."

Your Notes

5. Recap the Key Learning Points. Include the following points:

(a) Reaching consensus becomes increasingly difficult as the diversity of the group increases and the sensitivity of the issue increases.

(b) Our natural tendency in these situations may be to attack others' positions or to tell them why they are wrong and we are right.

(c) To work together in these situations requires that each member:

- Takes responsibility for trying to understand the other person's point of view first and then,
- Expresses their own opinion in such a way that others are open to listening.

6. Ask participants to complete the handout entitled Reflections (Handout H31.3) and to share their responses with one another in their individual groups.

7. Invite participants to share their individual learning in the larger group (if there is more than one group). (This step is a wind-up and reinforcement. You are not meant to ask each member to share, as they have already done so in their groups. Look for two or three volunteers who felt that their learning was particularly important or insightful.)

Your Notes

EARTHQUAKE— THE SCENARIO AND INSTRUCTIONS

THE SCENARIO

You work for a company called EduTours. You are one of a team of organizers and guides who have led a tour to an archaeological site on the Greek island of Crete. Six adventurous members of the tour chose to explore an underground tomb that could only be accessed by way of a narrow shaft. The group had just reached the tomb when the area experienced a mild earthquake. No one above or below ground was hurt. However, the shaft collapsed and water is now running into the tomb from an adjacent underground stream. You have called a rescue team. They have asked you to do only one thing—prepare a list of the names of the trapped individuals in the order they are to be rescued. This is to eliminate any confusion.

The water is rising quickly and it is possible that everyone will not get out. The rescue team is 30 minutes away.

INSTRUCTIONS

You must work as a group and come to agreement on the list of names to present to the rescue team. You have 30 minutes to complete your list.

(continued)

TOUR GROUP MEMBERS

In casual conversations, you have learned the following about the members of your group:

Pia　　　A university student, an only child and an opera singer who is described as having a brilliant future.

William　Retired. William came on the trip as a break from his full-time responsibility of caring for his wife who has Alzheimer's disease.

Sandra　Full time mother of two children, ages four and six. She and her husband Mark have taken this trip to celebrate their tenth wedding anniversary.

Mark　　Mark is a stockbroker, husband to Sandra and the father of her two children.

Sornsen　Sornsen is a research scientist with a pharmaceutical firm. He believes he may be close to finding a cure for AIDS.

Kathleen　Kathleen is taking a break from an intense investigation. She heads up an international team of aviation specialists who have been studying a series of plane crashes. While on this trip, she has been reflecting on her work and believes she has come up with the common denominator that may be causing the air disasters.

From *More Games Teams Play* by Leslie Bendaly © 2000, McGraw-Hill Ryerson.

OBSERVER'S GUIDE

Observe the discussion and decision-making process in your group giving particular attention to the following:

AIDING BEHAVIORS

Jot down a brief description of any behaviors that helped the group to move toward agreement, e.g. making an effort to understand one another's points of view.

_____

_____

_____

HINDERING BEHAVIORS

Jot down a brief description of any behaviors that hindered the group in their attempt to reach consensus, e.g. "shooting down" other's points of view.

_____

_____

_____

(continued)

From *More Games Teams Play* by Leslie Bendaly © 2000, McGraw-Hill Ryerson.

ENSURING EFFECTIVE DIALOGUE

Make note of each time a member makes an
effort to better understand another's point of view.

e.g. Can you tell us more?

I'm not sure I understand, can you explain . . .

Could you give us an example of what you mean . . .

Am I right in my understanding that . . ., etc.

_____

_____

_____

_____

PREVENTING DIALOGUE

Make note of each time a member responds to someone's
contribution by making a comment which hinders or prevents
effective dialogue.

e.g. Telling another group member that he or she is wrong.

Presenting one's own view and completely ignoring another's
input.

Explaining why one's own point of view is "more right."

_____

_____

_____

_____

REFLECTIONS

TIME REQUIRED: 15 minutes

Individually reflect on the Earthquake exercise and the subsequent discussion. Identify any of your own behaviors or comments that helped your group work more effectively together and/or move toward consensus.

_____

_____

_____

_____

_____

Identify any of your own behaviors or comments that may have hindered the group in its attempt to reach consensus.

_____

_____

_____

_____

Share your observations with one another.

THE UPDATED TEAM FITNESS TEST

OVERVIEW

Since first published in *Games Teams Play*, the "Team Fitness Test" has become standard equipment in many team facilitators' tool kits. The following is an expanded version of the original. The "Team Fitness Test" is not a magic wand, but it may be the closest thing to one that a team development facilitator can have in his or her repertoire. Teams that use the "Team Fitness Test" effectively experience a greatly accelerated team development process.

In order for a group to become a team, or for a team to become even better than it already is, the goals to be achieved must be clearly understood. Team members usually have ideas as to what could be better in their team. Few, however, have specific knowledge of what is required for high performance teamwork. Therefore, even when a team is consciously trying to improve, critical aspects that may be blocking team performance are often overlooked. The "Team Fitness Test" ensures that team members understand what creates high performance teamwork and focuses the team's attention on the areas that will bring the greatest return.

Team development is most effective when a system that supports an ongoing development process is in place. The results of the "Team Fitness Test" prioritize development needs and provide a benchmark. The system is a simple one involving the following steps:

1. Examining the results of the "Team Fitness Test".

From *More Games Teams Play* by Leslie Bendaly © 2000, McGraw-Hill Ryerson.

> **Your Notes**

2. Identifying and celebrating strengths.

3. Identifying opportunities for growth.

4. Acting on the opportunities for growth.

Teams beginning the development process should use the "Team Fitness Test" every two to three months to monitor their progress. As the team reaches levels of high performance, they can continue to use the "Team Fitness Test" to help maintain their performance level and to further enhance it. Some apply the test every six months, others once a year if the team life-line extends that far.

One of the greatest benefits of the fitness test is that it quickly turns the ownership for the development of the group over to the team. When the facilitator shares the data, it is important to emphasize that this is the team's view of itself, its strengths and opportunities: "Here is how you see your team."

When examining the responses and discussing opportunities for growth, once again, the team members' responsibility is obvious. Asking "What do you believe you can do to strengthen this element?" will lead to specific team agreements and commitments to action which must be followed up and reinforced regularly. Any workouts that the facilitator selects to strengthen a specific element also leads the team toward clarifying agreements or commitments to action, i.e., more effective teamwork.

PREPARATION

1. Prior to the workshop, distribute copies of the Updated "Team Fitness Test" (Handout H.2) and the Team Fitness Scoring Sheet (Handout H.3) to each team member. Ask them to record their responses on the "Team Fitness Scoring Sheet" (Handout H.3), and to forward it to you, keeping a copy for themselves. Ask them to bring this copy to the workshop.

2. Assure team members that their responses are confidential and that names are not required.

Your Notes

3. Compile the data. For each element or column (indicated by the Roman numerals), add all the scores and divide by the number of responses.

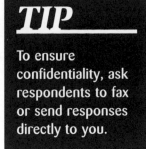

TIP

To ensure confidentiality, ask respondents to fax or send responses directly to you.

Record team scores and team ranking on the Team Fitness Interpretation Sheet (Handout H.4).

4. Note the range of scores (i.e., lowest and highest) for each element as indicated. This is particularly important if responses differ greatly or if one or two responses are considerably higher or lower than the rest and so affect the average.

5. Examine the lowest scores and look for statements that were consistently given a low rating. From this information, select appropriate games or activities (see Index on page xix).

6. Plan how the team can most productively discuss the results.

WORKSHOP STEPS

1. Distribute copies of the "Team Fitness Elements" handout (Handout H.1).

2. Display Overhead T.1 and discuss the "Team Fitness Elements" to ensure that each group member understands the terms.

3. Distribute copies of the "Team Fitness Interpretation Sheet" (Handout H.4).

4. Ask participants to complete the columns headed "Your Score" and "Your Ranking" for each of the six elements, by referring to their own copy of the "Team Fitness Scoring Sheet" (Handout H.3). Note that each column corresponds to one of the six Team Fitness Elements.

5. Interpret the results. Teams seldom just happen, they are developed. Therefore,

Your Notes

unless a team has made a conscious effort to develop, it is unlikely to produce scores of over 18. If a team has not been focusing on its development and produces high scores (an uncommon scenario), the facilitator must ask the team to ensure that their self-examination has been honest.

6. Discuss the results from the "Team Fitness Test".

   (a) Recognize the team's strengths based on the elements that received the highest scores.

   (b) For each element that offers opportunities for improvement, ask the following two questions:

   - Why do you think the _____ element is relatively weak?

   - What can you, the team members, do to strengthen this element?

7. Identify points of agreement.

8. Recap points of agreement and commitments to action.

OUTCOME

The benefits to be gained from taking the "Team Fitness Test" include acquiring an understanding of team strengths and opportunities for improvement, increased ownership on the part of team members for team development, and team commitments to action to increase team effectiveness.

Your Notes

TEAM FITNESS ELEMENTS

- Shared Leadership

- Group Work Skills

- Climate

- Cohesiveness

- Team Members' Contribution

- Change Compatibility

Handout
H.1

TEAM FITNESS ELEMENTS

Each of these elements is crucial to team fitness. Each affects the strength of the others.

SHARED LEADERSHIP

Shared leadership requires that:

• Team members are well informed.

• Each member fully participates.

• Each member has an equal voice. (In some decisions some members may have more influence than others because of their particular experience, skills, etc.; however, all input is valued.)

• Team members share decision-making as appropriate.

GROUP WORK SKILLS

A team's ability to work effectively in a meeting setting is critical to its effectiveness outside of the meeting. If the best decisions are not made, or if true consensus is not achieved, a team cannot function at its best.

The Group Work Skills element reflects the quality of decision-making and problem solving, consensus reaching, meeting management and facilitation. Synergistic and productive meetings are reflected in the energy and success displayed in a team's day-to-day operations.

(continued)

CLIMATE

Climate refers generally to how members feel about the way the team functions, including their level of comfort with team norms of behavior. If the climate is not positive, honesty and openness are lacking and team members may not fully trust one another. The communication process then requires attention.

COHESIVENESS

Cohesiveness refers to the degree to which the group pulls together. Cohesiveness requires agreement and commitment to **what** the team is in place to achieve (mandate, goals, and objectives), as well as **how** it will achieve them (values, priorities, and procedures).

TEAM MEMBERS' CONTRIBUTION

Team members' contribution refers to the team members' understanding of what is expected of them as team members and the degree to which they fulfill that expectation. Expectations of team members include that they share information; communicate openly with one another; share the load; actively participate; demonstrate commitment to the team's goals and values; take equal responsibility for the success of the team; and recognize the degree to which individual behaviors affect the effectiveness of the team.

CHANGE COMPATIBILITY

The team that thrives today must be able to maintain high performance in an environment of accelerated and constant change.

Change compatibility requires:

- Receptivity to change.
- Adaptability to change.
- Effectiveness evaluation of opportunities for change.

THE UPDATED TEAM FITNESS TEST

Read each of the following statements with your team in mind. Rate each of the statements as it applies to your team using the following rating scale:

4—This statement definitely applies to our team.

3—This statement applies to our team most of the time.

2—This statement is occasionally true for our team.

1—This statement does not describe our team at all.

Enter the score that you believe is appropriate for each statement beside its number on the "Team Fitness Scoring Sheet" (Handout H.3).

1. Each team member has an equal voice.

2. We leave our meetings with a sense of accomplishment.

3. Team members know they can depend on each other.

4. Our mandate, goals and objectives are clear and agreed to.

5. Team members readily help one another/share the load.

(continued)

From *More Games Teams Play* by Leslie Bendaly © 2000, McGraw-Hill Ryerson.

6. Our team is open to new ideas.

7. Team members see participation as a responsibility.

8. Members make team meetings a priority.

9. There is a feeling of openness and trust in our team.

10. We have strong, agreed upon beliefs about how to achieve success.

11. Team members look for opportunities to enhance team performance.

12. Once a change is implemented in our team, it sticks.

13. Input from team members is used whenever possible.

14. We all participate fully in team meetings.

15. Team members do not allow personal priorities/agendas to hinder team effectiveness.

16. Our roles are clearly defined and accepted as defined by all team members.

17. Team members keep each other well informed.

18. We take a positive attitude toward change with which we may not agree but over which we have no control.

(continued)

From *More Games Teams Play* by Leslie Bendaly © 2000, McGraw-Hill Ryerson.

19. The right people are involved in the right decisions.

20. In team meetings we stay on track and on time.

21. Team members feel free to give their honest opinions.

22. If we were each asked to list team priorities, our lists would be very similar.

23. Team members take initiative to put forth ideas and concerns.

24. We are receptive to change but do not get caught up in change for the sake of change.

25. Team members are kept well informed.

26. When sharing a decision, we come to consensus easily.

27. Team members respect each other.

28. When making decisions, we agree on priorities.

29. Each team member pulls his or her weight.

30. Our team implements change effectively.

TEAM FITNESS SCORING SHEET

I		II		III		IV		V		VI	
Statement Number	Score	Statement Number	Score	Statement Number	Score	Statement Number	Score	Statement Number	Score	Statement Number	Score
1.		2.		3.		4.		5.		6.	
7.		8.		9.		10.		11.		12.	
13.		14.		15.		16.		17.		18.	
19.		20.		21.		22.		23.		24.	
25.		26.		27.		28.		29.		30.	
Total		Total		Total		Total		Total		Total	

From *More Games Teams Play* by Leslie Bendaly © 2000, McGraw-Hill Ryerson.

TEAM FITNESS INTERPRETATION SHEET

Column	Your Score	Your Ranking	Team Average	Team Ranking	Range of Scores*	Team Fitness Element
I						Shared Leadership
II						Group Work Skills
III						Climate
IV						Cohesiveness
V						Team Member's Contribution
VI						Change Compatibility

*lowest score and highest score

Ranking—Your lowest score will be **ranked** number 1, second lowest score number 2, etc.

MORE Best-selling TRAINING PRODUCTS from McGraw-Hill Ryerson